THIS BOOK

BELONGS TO

....

Thank you for Purchasing my book and taking the time to read it from front to back. I am always grateful when a reader chooses my work and I hope you enjoyed it!

With the vast selection available online, I am touched that you chose to be purchasing my work and take valuable time out of your life to read it. My hope is that you feel you made the right decision.

I very much would like to know what you thought of the book. Please take the time to write an honest and informative review on Amazon.com. Your experience and opinions will be of great benefit to me and those readers looking to make an informed choice.

With much thanks.

Table of Contents

SUMMARY

What is the Amigurumi? What is the Amigurumi Crochet?: Amigurumi is a Japanese art form that involves creating small, stuffed animals or objects using crochet techniques. The word "amigurumi" is derived from the Japanese words "ami," meaning crocheted or knitted, and "nuigurumi," meaning stuffed doll.

Amigurumi crochet is a specific type of crochet that is used to create these adorable and often whimsical creatures. It involves using a small hook and fine yarn to create tight stitches, resulting in a dense and sturdy fabric. The technique typically involves working in continuous rounds, rather than rows, to create a seamless and smooth finish.

The process of making amigurumi begins with selecting a pattern or design. There are countless patterns available online, in books, and through various crochet communities. These patterns provide step-by-step instructions on how to create each individual part of the amigurumi, such as the head, body, arms, and legs. They also include details on how to assemble the pieces and add any additional features, such as eyes, noses, or clothing.

Once the pattern is chosen, the crocheter selects the appropriate yarn and hook size. The yarn used for amigurumi is typically a lightweight, acrylic or cotton blend, as this allows for tight stitches and easy shaping. The hook size is usually smaller than what would be used for traditional crochet projects, such as blankets or scarves, to achieve the desired tightness and detail.

The crocheter then begins by creating a magic ring, which is a technique used to start working in the round. From there, they follow the pattern instructions to create each individual part of the amigurumi. This often involves increasing and decreasing stitches to shape the pieces and create the desired form. The crocheter must pay close attention to the pattern and stitch count to ensure that the amigurumi is symmetrical and well-proportioned.

Once all the parts are crocheted, they are then assembled using a yarn needle and thread. This involves sewing the pieces together, stuffing them with fiberfill or other stuffing material, and adding any additional features, such as eyes or buttons. The crocheter can also choose to embroider details onto the amigurumi, such as facial expressions or decorative elements.

Amigurumi crochet is a popular craft that has gained a significant following worldwide. It allows for creativity and self-expression, as crocheters can customize their amigurumi by choosing different

The Origin and Popularity of Amigurumi Crochet: Amigurumi crochet is a Japanese art form that involves creating small, stuffed animals or objects using crochet techniques. The word "amigurumi" is derived from the Japanese words "ami," meaning crocheted or knitted, and "nuigurumi," meaning stuffed doll. This craft has gained immense popularity worldwide in recent years, captivating both crochet enthusiasts and those who appreciate cute and whimsical handmade creations.

The origin of amigurumi can be traced back to Japan in the early 20th century. Traditionally, amigurumi dolls were made using knitting techniques, but crochet became the preferred method due to its versatility and ability to create more intricate designs. The craft gained momentum in the 1980s when crochet patterns for amigurumi dolls started appearing in Japanese craft magazines. These patterns were often accompanied by detailed instructions and illustrations, making it easier for crafters to replicate the designs.

The appeal of amigurumi lies in its ability to bring inanimate objects to life through the use of yarn and a crochet hook. Crafters can create a wide variety of characters, ranging from animals and mythical creatures to food items and everyday objects. The possibilities are endless, limited only by one's imagination. The small size of amigurumi makes them perfect for collecting, gifting, or using as decorative items.

One of the reasons for the popularity of amigurumi is its accessibility. Unlike other crafts that may require specialized tools or materials, amigurumi can be created with just a crochet hook, yarn, and some stuffing. This makes it an ideal craft for beginners or those looking for a portable and affordable hobby. Additionally, the internet has played a significant role in the spread of amigurumi, with countless blogs, websites, and social media platforms dedicated to sharing patterns, tutorials, and inspiration.

Amigurumi has also gained recognition in the art world, with exhibitions and galleries showcasing the intricate and imaginative creations of talented amigurumi artists. The craft has evolved beyond simple dolls, with artists pushing the boundaries of design and incorporating various techniques such as embroidery, beading, and wirework into their creations. This has elevated amigurumi from a craft to an art form, attracting a wider audience and garnering appreciation from both the crafting community and art enthusiasts.

In recent years, amigurumi has become a global phenomenon, with enthusiasts and collectors from all corners of the world embracing this charming craft.

Understanding Crochet Tools and Materials: Crochet is a popular craft that involves creating fabric by interlocking loops of yarn or thread using a crochet hook. To successfully engage in this craft, it is essential to have a good understanding of the various crochet tools and materials that are used.

One of the most important tools in crochet is the crochet hook. These hooks come in various sizes, ranging from small to large, and are made from different materials such as aluminum, plastic, or wood. The size of the crochet hook determines the size of the stitches and ultimately the size of the finished project. It is important to choose the right size hook for the yarn or thread being used to ensure that the stitches are neither too tight nor too loose.

Another essential tool in crochet is a pair of scissors. These are used to cut the yarn or thread when changing colors or finishing a project. It is important to have a sharp pair of scissors that can easily cut through the yarn without fraying or damaging it.

Yarn or thread is the main material used in crochet. There are countless options available when it comes to choosing yarn, including different fibers, weights, and colors. The type of yarn used can greatly affect the look and feel of the finished project. For beginners, it is recommended to start with a medium-weight yarn in a light color, as it is easier to work with and mistakes are less noticeable.

In addition to yarn, other materials that may be used in crochet include buttons, beads, and ribbons. These embellishments can be added to projects to enhance their appearance and add a personal touch. It is important to choose materials that are compatible with the yarn being used and that can withstand the wear and tear of everyday use.

To keep track of stitches and patterns, it is helpful to have a set of stitch markers. These small, removable markers are placed on the stitches to mark specific points in the pattern. They can be used to indicate the beginning of a round, the location of a stitch increase or decrease, or any other important points in the pattern. Stitch markers come in various shapes and sizes, and it is important to choose ones that are easy to use and do not snag the yarn.

Lastly, a tapestry needle is an essential tool for finishing crochet projects. This needle has a large eye and a blunt tip, making it easy to weave in loose ends and sew pieces together.

Basic Crochet Stitches and Techniques Used in Amigurumi: Amigurumi, the Japanese art of crocheting small stuffed animals and creatures, has gained immense popularity in recent years. Whether you're a beginner or an experienced crocheter, it's important to have a good understanding of the basic crochet stitches and techniques used in amigurumi. These stitches and techniques form the foundation of creating adorable and intricate amigurumi designs.

One of the most commonly used stitches in amigurumi is the single crochet stitch. This stitch is simple yet versatile, making it perfect for creating the tight and compact stitches required for amigurumi projects. To work a single crochet stitch, insert your hook into the designated stitch, yarn over, and pull through a loop. Yarn over again and pull through both loops on your hook. Repeat this process for each stitch, creating a neat and uniform fabric.

Another important stitch in amigurumi is the magic ring or adjustable ring. This technique is used to create a tight and seamless starting point for your amigurumi project. To make a magic ring, hold the end of your yarn between your thumb and middle finger, leaving a small tail. Wrap the yarn around your fingers, creating a loop. Insert your hook through the loop, yarn over, and pull through a loop. Then, chain one to secure the ring. This technique allows you to easily adjust the size of the ring by pulling the tail end of the yarn.

Increasing and decreasing stitches are essential techniques in amigurumi, as they help shape your creations. To increase stitches, simply work two single crochet stitches into the same stitch. This creates an additional stitch and adds width to your project. To decrease stitches, insert your hook into the next stitch, yarn over, and pull through a loop. Then, insert your hook into the following stitch, yarn over, and pull through a loop. Yarn over again and pull through all three loops on your hook. This technique helps create curves and contours in your amigurumi designs.

In addition to these basic stitches and techniques, it's important to have a good understanding of color changes, embroidery, and finishing techniques. Color changes allow you to create intricate patterns and designs in your amigurumi. Simply switch to a different color of yarn at the desired point in your project. Embroidery techniques, such as adding eyes, noses, and other details, bring your amigurumi to life.

Materials and Tools for Amigurumi Crochet: Amigurumi crochet is a popular craft that involves creating small stuffed animals or dolls using crochet techniques. To get started with amigurumi crochet, you will need a few essential materials and tools.

First and foremost, you will need yarn. When choosing yarn for amigurumi, it is important to select a type that is suitable for the project. Typically, a medium weight yarn, also known as worsted weight or aran weight, is recommended for amigurumi. This type of yarn is easy to work with and provides a good balance between durability and softness. Additionally, acrylic yarn is often preferred for amigurumi as it is machine washable and retains its shape well.

In addition to yarn, you will also need crochet hooks. The size of the crochet hook you use will depend on the thickness of the yarn you have chosen. It is important to match the hook size to the yarn weight to ensure that your stitches are the correct size and tension. Most amigurumi projects require a smaller hook size, typically ranging from 2.5mm to 4mm. It is a good idea to have a set of crochet hooks in various sizes to accommodate different projects.

Another essential tool for amigurumi crochet is a pair of scissors. You will need scissors to cut the yarn and trim any excess ends. It is important to have a sharp pair of scissors that can easily cut through the yarn without fraying or damaging it.

Furthermore, you will need a yarn needle or tapestry needle. This needle is used for weaving in loose ends and sewing different parts of the amigurumi together. A yarn needle with a large eye is recommended as it allows you to easily thread the yarn through.

Safety eyes or buttons are often used to give amigurumi toys a more realistic and expressive look. Safety eyes are plastic eyes that can be securely attached to the amigurumi using a washer or a plastic backing. Alternatively, you can use buttons as eyes, but it is important to ensure that they are securely sewn on to prevent any choking hazards, especially if the amigurumi is intended for young children.

Lastly, stuffing is needed to give the amigurumi its shape and make it soft and cuddly. Polyester fiberfill is commonly used as stuffing for amigurumi as it is lightweight, hypoallergenic, and retains its shape well.

Selecting the Right Yarn and Colors of Amigurumi Crochet: When it comes to creating amigurumi crochet projects, selecting the right yarn and colors is crucial in achieving the desired results. The choice of yarn not only affects the overall appearance of the amigurumi but also determines its durability and ease of maintenance.

One of the first considerations when choosing yarn for amigurumi is the fiber content. Acrylic yarn is a popular choice for beginners and experienced crocheters alike due to its affordability, wide range of colors, and easy care. It is also a great option for creating amigurumi toys that will be frequently handled or washed, as it is machine washable and retains its shape well.

Another popular choice for amigurumi is cotton yarn. Cotton has a soft and natural feel, making it ideal for creating cuddly and huggable amigurumi toys. It is also hypoallergenic, making it suitable for those with sensitive skin or allergies. However, cotton yarn tends to have less stretch than acrylic, so it may require a larger crochet hook or tighter stitches to achieve the desired shape.

Wool yarn is another option for amigurumi, particularly for those looking for a more luxurious and warm feel. Wool has excellent stitch definition and is known for its ability to hold its shape well. However, it is important to note that wool can be more expensive than other yarn options and may require special care, such as hand washing and blocking.

In addition to the fiber content, the weight or thickness of the yarn is also an important consideration. Amigurumi projects typically require a lightweight yarn, such as sport or DK (double knitting) weight, to achieve the desired size and proportions. Using a heavier yarn may result in a larger and bulkier amigurumi, while using a lighter yarn may create a smaller and more delicate toy.

When it comes to selecting colors for amigurumi, the possibilities are endless. The choice of colors can greatly impact the overall look and feel of the finished project. Bright and vibrant colors are often used for creating playful and whimsical amigurumi toys, while pastel shades can give a more delicate and dreamy appearance. It is also common to use a combination of colors to add depth and dimension to the amigurumi, such as using different shades for the body, limbs, and facial features.

Crochet Hooks and Finding Your Preferred Size of Amigurumi Crochet: When it comes to crocheting amigurumi, one of the most important tools you'll need is a crochet hook. The crochet hook is what you'll use to create the stitches that form the body and details of your amigurumi. However, not all crochet hooks are created equal, and finding the right size for your amigurumi projects is crucial for achieving the desired outcome.

Crochet hooks come in various sizes, ranging from small to large. The size of a crochet hook is determined by the diameter of its shaft, with smaller numbers indicating a smaller hook and larger numbers indicating a larger hook. The most commonly used sizes for amigurumi range from 2.25mm to 4.5mm, although some crocheters may prefer larger or smaller hooks depending on their personal preferences and the type of yarn they are using.

Choosing the right size crochet hook for your amigurumi project is important for several reasons. Firstly, the size of the hook will determine the size of the stitches you create. Using a smaller hook will result in tighter stitches, while using a larger hook will create looser stitches. The size of the stitches will ultimately affect the size and overall appearance of your amigurumi. If you want your amigurumi to be small and compact, you'll want to use a smaller hook. On the other hand, if you want your amigurumi to be larger and more floppy, a larger hook would be more suitable.

Secondly, the size of the hook will also affect the tension of your stitches. Tension refers to how tightly or loosely you hold the yarn as you crochet. Some crocheters naturally have a looser tension, while others have a tighter tension. The size of the hook can help compensate for your natural tension. If you have a looser tension, using a smaller hook can help create tighter stitches. Conversely, if you have a tighter tension, using a larger hook can help create looser stitches.

To find your preferred size of crochet hook for amigurumi, it's important to experiment and practice with different sizes. Start by trying out the commonly used sizes mentioned earlier and see how they work for you. Pay attention to the size and tension of your stitches and how they affect the overall appearance of your amigurumi. You may find that you prefer a slightly smaller or larger hook than the recommended sizes, and that's perfectly fine. Croch

Essential Accessories: Stuffing, Eyes, and More of Amigurumi Crochet: When it comes to amigurumi crochet, there are a few essential accessories that every crocheter should have in their arsenal. These accessories not only enhance the overall look of your amigurumi creations but also add a touch of personality and charm to them. From stuffing to eyes and more, let's delve into the world of essential amigurumi crochet accessories.

First and foremost, stuffing is a crucial accessory for amigurumi crochet. It is what gives your creations their shape and volume, transforming them from flat pieces of crochet into adorable stuffed toys. There are various types of stuffing available, such as polyester fiberfill or cotton stuffing, each with its own unique qualities. Polyester fiberfill is a popular choice as it is lightweight, hypoallergenic, and retains its shape well. On the other hand, cotton stuffing is a natural option that provides a softer and more organic feel to your amigurumi. Whichever type you choose, make sure to stuff your amigurumi firmly but not too tightly, allowing it to maintain its cuddly and huggable nature.

Next on the list of essential accessories are the eyes. The eyes are what bring your amigurumi to life, giving them a personality and making them more relatable. There are various options for amigurumi eyes, including safety eyes, plastic eyes, or embroidered eyes. Safety eyes are a popular choice as they are easy to attach and provide a secure and child-safe option. They come in different sizes and colors, allowing you to customize the look of your amigurumi. Plastic eyes, on the other hand, offer a more realistic appearance and are often used for amigurumi that aim for a lifelike representation. Lastly, embroidered eyes are a great option for those who prefer a more handmade and whimsical look. They can be stitched using embroidery floss or yarn, allowing for endless creativity and customization.

In addition to stuffing and eyes, there are a few more accessories that can elevate your amigurumi crochet projects. One such accessory is a crochet hook set. A good set of crochet hooks in various sizes ensures that you have the right tool for every project. It allows you to achieve the desired tension and stitch definition, resulting in beautifully crafted amigurumi. Another useful accessory is a stitch marker. Stitch markers help you keep track of your rounds or specific stitches, preventing any confusion or mistakes along the way.

Basic Techniques and Tips for Amigurumi Crochet: Amigurumi crochet is a popular craft that involves creating small stuffed toys or characters using crochet techniques. If you're new to amigurumi crochet or looking to improve your skills, here are some basic techniques and tips to help you get started or enhance your creations.

1. Choosing the Right Yarn and Hook Size:

Selecting the appropriate yarn and hook size is crucial for achieving the desired outcome in amigurumi crochet. Generally, a lightweight yarn such as sport or DK weight works best, as it allows for tighter stitches and better definition. As for the hook size, it should be smaller than what is typically recommended for the chosen yarn weight. This helps create a dense fabric that prevents stuffing from showing through.

2. Magic Ring Technique:

The magic ring technique is commonly used to start amigurumi projects in a seamless and adjustable manner. It involves creating a loop with the yarn, inserting the hook through the loop, and working the initial stitches into the loop. This technique allows you to tighten the center of your project by pulling the tail end of the yarn, resulting in a neat and closed starting point.

3. Single Crochet Stitch:

The single crochet stitch is the foundation of amigurumi crochet. It creates a tight and compact fabric that is ideal for stuffing. Mastering this stitch is essential for creating smooth and even amigurumi pieces. Practice maintaining consistent tension and stitch size to achieve a professional finish.

4. Increasing and Decreasing:

To shape your amigurumi, you'll need to learn how to increase and decrease stitches. Increasing involves adding extra stitches in a single stitch, while decreasing involves combining stitches to reduce the stitch count. These techniques allow you to create curves, angles, and other intricate shapes in your amigurumi designs.

5. Stuffing and Assembly:

Proper stuffing and assembly are crucial for giving your amigurumi a professional and polished look. Use polyester fiberfill or other suitable stuffing materials to fill your amigurumi evenly, ensuring there are no lumps or gaps. Take care not to overstuff, as it can distort the shape of your creation. Additionally, pay attention to the placement and attachment of limbs, eyes, and other embellishments to achieve a well-balanced and secure finished product.

6. Adding Details:

Adding details to your amigurumi can bring them to life and make them more visually appealing. Consider using embroidery techniques to create facial features, such as eyes, nose

Increasing and Decreasing Stitches in Amigurumi Crochet: Amigurumi crochet is a popular technique used to create adorable stuffed toys and characters. One of the key elements in amigurumi crochet is the use of increasing and decreasing stitches to shape the project.

Increasing stitches are used to make the amigurumi project wider or larger. This is achieved by adding extra stitches in a single round. There are several ways to increase stitches in amigurumi crochet, including the single crochet increase (also known as sc inc), half double crochet increase (hdc inc), and double crochet increase (dc inc). Each increase stitch adds one extra stitch to the round, allowing the project to gradually expand.

On the other hand, decreasing stitches are used to make the amigurumi project narrower or smaller. This is done by eliminating stitches in a single round. Similar to increasing stitches, there are different methods to decrease stitches in amigurumi crochet, such as the single crochet decrease (sc dec), half double crochet decrease (hdc dec), and double crochet decrease (dc dec). Each decrease stitch removes one stitch from the round, resulting in a more compact shape.

Understanding how to properly increase and decrease stitches is crucial in amigurumi crochet, as it allows you to create the desired shape and proportions for your project. It is important to follow the pattern instructions carefully, as they will specify which type of increase or decrease stitch to use in each round.

When increasing stitches, it is important to evenly distribute the additional stitches around the round to maintain a symmetrical shape. This can be achieved by spacing out the increase stitches evenly or by following a specific pattern provided in the instructions. It is also important to count your stitches after each round to ensure that you have added the correct number of stitches.

When decreasing stitches, it is important to pay attention to the placement of the decrease stitches to maintain the desired shape. Depending on the pattern, you may need to decrease stitches in a specific sequence or at specific intervals. It is crucial to count your stitches after each round to ensure that you have decreased the correct number of stitches.

In addition to shaping the project, increasing and decreasing stitches also play a role in creating texture and design elements in amigurumi crochet. By strategically placing increase and decrease stitches, you can create curves, angles, and other intricate details in your amigurumi project.

Techniques for Stuffing and Shaping Your Amigurumi Crochet: Amigurumi crochet is a popular craft that involves creating small stuffed toys or characters using crochet techniques. One of the key aspects of amigurumi is the stuffing and shaping of the finished piece. This is what gives the toy its three-dimensional form and makes it soft and cuddly.

There are several techniques that can be used to stuff and shape amigurumi crochet projects. The first step is to choose the right type of stuffing material. Polyester fiberfill is commonly used for amigurumi as it is lightweight, soft, and hypoallergenic. It can be easily manipulated to achieve the desired shape and density.

To begin stuffing the amigurumi, start by filling the limbs and body first. This helps to create a solid base and ensures that the stuffing is evenly distributed. Use small amounts of stuffing at a time and gently push it into the desired areas using a stuffing tool or the end of a crochet hook. Take care not to overstuff, as this can distort the shape of the amigurumi.

When stuffing the head, it is important to pay attention to the facial features. Use smaller amounts of stuffing and shape it carefully to create the desired expression. For example, if you want a round and chubby face, add more stuffing to the cheeks. If you want a more defined snout or muzzle, shape the stuffing accordingly.

To achieve a smooth and even finish, it is recommended to stuff the amigurumi firmly but not too tightly. This helps to prevent lumps and bumps from forming. Take breaks during the stuffing process to check the shape and make adjustments as needed.

Once the amigurumi is fully stuffed, it is time to shape it. This can be done by gently manipulating the stuffed parts with your hands. For example, you can shape the limbs to create a natural bend or curve. You can also shape the body to give it a more rounded or elongated appearance.

To create more intricate shapes or details, you can use additional materials such as wire or pipe cleaners. These can be inserted into the amigurumi to provide structure and support. For example, if you want the amigurumi to have poseable arms or legs, you can insert wire into the limbs before stuffing them.

In addition to shaping the amigurumi, you can also add finishing touches to enhance its appearance.

Decoding Abbreviations and Symbols of Amigurumi Crochet:

Amigurumi crochet has gained immense popularity in recent years, with its adorable and intricate designs capturing the hearts of crafters worldwide. However, for beginners or those unfamiliar with the craft, deciphering the abbreviations and symbols used in amigurumi patterns can be quite daunting. Understanding these abbreviations and symbols is crucial for successfully creating amigurumi projects, as they provide essential instructions for each stitch and technique.

When it comes to amigurumi crochet patterns, abbreviations are commonly used to represent different stitches and techniques. These abbreviations are often a combination of letters and numbers, and they serve as a shorthand way of conveying instructions. For example, "sc" stands for single crochet, "dc" for double crochet, and "inc" for increase. By familiarizing yourself with these abbreviations, you can easily follow the pattern instructions and create the desired stitches.

In addition to abbreviations, amigurumi crochet patterns also utilize symbols to represent specific actions or techniques. These symbols are visual representations of stitches and are often used in charts or diagrams. For instance, a small "x" may indicate a single crochet stitch, while a "+" symbol may represent a double crochet stitch. Understanding these symbols is crucial for accurately interpreting the pattern and achieving the desired outcome.

To decode the abbreviations and symbols of amigurumi crochet, it is essential to refer to a comprehensive guide or resource specifically designed for this purpose. Many crochet books and online tutorials provide detailed explanations of common abbreviations and symbols used in amigurumi patterns. These resources often include step-by-step instructions, illustrations, and even video tutorials to help you grasp the concepts more easily.

When starting a new amigurumi project, it is advisable to carefully read through the pattern instructions and make note of any unfamiliar abbreviations or symbols. By referring to your chosen guide or resource, you can quickly identify and understand the meaning behind each abbreviation or symbol. This will enable you to confidently proceed with your project, knowing that you are correctly interpreting the instructions.

Furthermore, practice is key to becoming proficient in decoding amigurumi crochet abbreviations and symbols. As you work on more projects and encounter different patterns, you will become more familiar with the common abbreviations and symbols used in amigurumi crochet.

Tips for Keeping Track of Your Progress in Amigurumi Crochet: Amigurumi crochet is a popular craft that involves creating small stuffed animals or dolls using crochet techniques. It can be a fun and rewarding hobby, but it can also be challenging to keep track of your progress, especially if you are working on multiple projects at once. However, with a few tips and tricks, you can easily stay organized and monitor your progress in amigurumi crochet.

Firstly, it is essential to keep a record of the patterns you are working on. This can be done by creating a physical or digital folder where you store all the patterns you have used or plan to use. You can print out the patterns and keep them in a binder or save them as PDF files on your computer or smartphone. By having all your patterns in one place, you can easily refer back to them whenever needed and keep track of the projects you have completed.

Next, consider using a project journal or notebook to document your progress. This can be a simple notebook where you jot down the details of each project, such as the pattern name, yarn used, hook size, and any modifications you made. You can also include notes on the techniques or stitches you struggled with or found particularly enjoyable. This journal can serve as a reference for future projects and help you remember the specific details of each amigurumi you have made.

Another helpful tip is to take photos of your work at different stages of completion. This not only allows you to visually track your progress but also serves as a visual reminder of the techniques and stitches you used. You can create a dedicated folder on your phone or computer to store these progress photos, making it easy to compare your current project to previous ones. Additionally, sharing these photos on social media platforms or online crochet communities can provide you with valuable feedback and encouragement from fellow amigurumi enthusiasts.

In addition to documenting your progress, it is also important to keep track of the materials you use. This includes noting down the brand, color, and type of yarn, as well as the specific hook size. By keeping a record of the materials used for each project, you can easily replicate successful combinations or avoid using materials that did not work well for a particular amigurumi. This information can also be helpful when purchasing new supplies or when someone asks for recommendations on yarn or hooks.

Lastly, consider setting goals for yourself and tracking your progress towards achieving them. This can be as simple as aiming to complete a certain number of amigurumi projects within a specific

PART 1

AMIGURUMI ESSENTIALS

Are you ready to start your amigurumi journey? Don't worry if you're feeling a bit overwhelmed. I've been there. Learning a new skill can feel daunting, but I promise you that with some patience—and my help—you'll be creating adorable stuffed toys in no time.

In this part, you will learn about the tools, stitches, and techniques used to create amigurumi. You'll learn the foundational skills of amigurumi, including how to choose your hook and yarn, read a pattern, master the basic crochet stitches, and assemble your toy. Let's dive in together.

Adorable Amigurumi

Amigurumi is a portmanteau of two Japanese terms: *ami*, which means crocheted or knitted, and *nuigurumi*, which means a stuffed doll. Amigurumi come in all shapes, sizes, and styles, but they all have one thing in common: They're cute. I can't help but smile when I see an amigurumi toy, and if you've picked up this book, I bet you feel the same way. There's nothing quite like the satisfaction of finishing a project and seeing a cuddly stuffed animal stare up at you.

Over the years, I've spoken to many people—crocheters and non-crocheters alike—who have told me that amigurumi is too complicated for them. My response is always the same: If you can do a single crochet stitch, you can make amigurumi.

Once you grasp the mechanics of putting hook to yarn, the rest will follow. Some of the cutest patterns are also the easiest to make, and there is no shortage of beginner amigurumi patterns for you to choose from. The twenty patterns in this book are perfect for beginners and will provide you with a firm grounding in the basics of amigurumi. Once you've worked through these projects, a whole world of amigurumi will open up to you, and you won't want to stop.

Set Up Your Supplies

Before we get started, you'll need to gather a few essential supplies. In this section, you'll learn about the basic tools needed to complete your toys, including crochet hooks, yarn, stuffing, and other accessories. The patterns in this book are all made using a size G-6 (4.00 mm) crochet hook and worsted weight yarn. No idea what those terms mean? Read on to find out.

Getting Hooked

The first and most important tool in any crocheter's kit is the crochet hook. There are three main considerations when choosing a crochet hook: size, style, and material.

HOOK SIZE

The hook size you choose will depend on the project you're making and the size of the yarn. Typically, the required hook size for a project will be stated in the pattern. Crochet hook sizes are represented by either a number or a letter, depending on the country and brand. Each hook also has a metric size, which is the diameter of the shaft in millimeters. For example, a 4.00 mm hook is called a G-6 hook in the United States and a #8 hook in the United Kingdom. Confused? Don't worry, I've included a handy chart so you can compare.

CROCHET HOOK SIZE

METRIC	US	UK
2.25 mm	B-1	13
2.75 mm	C-2	12
3.25 mm	D-3	10
3.50 mm	E-4	-
3.75 mm	F-5	9
4.00 mm	G-6	8
5.00 mm	H-8	6
5.50 mm	I-9	5
6.00 mm	J-10	4
6.50 mm	K-10.5	3
8.00 mm	L-11	0
9.00 mm	M-13	00
10.00 mm	N-15	000
12.00 mm	P-16	-

HOOK STYLE

There are two main types of hook style: inline (Susan Bates brand) and tapered (Boye brand). Neither style is better than the other, and your choice simply depends on which style feels most comfortable for you.

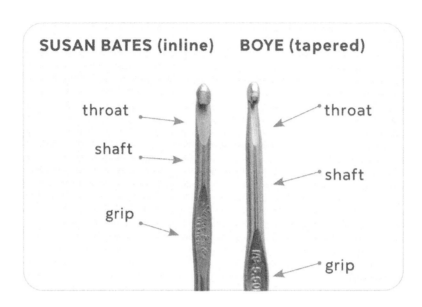

HOOK MATERIAL

Crochet hooks are made from a variety of materials, including aluminum, stainless steel, plastic, and bamboo. Aluminum is the most common hook material and is a great choice for beginners, as aluminum hooks are affordable and easy to find at craft stores. Plastic hooks are the cheapest option and are very lightweight, but not as smooth as aluminum hooks. They are best used for bulky projects. Wood and bamboo hooks are typically more expensive options.

For beginners, I suggest picking up a couple of aluminum hooks to get started. As you improve and get more serious about your crocheting, consider purchasing a set of ergonomic crochet hooks. Ergonomic hooks feature a thick, soft rubber handle that is easier to hold and helps alleviate the hand pain that can result from long crocheting sessions. These hooks are a bit pricier than simple aluminum hooks, but your hands will thank you.

All about Yarn

Choosing yarn is one of the most fun parts of crocheting, and the options available are nearly endless. Yarn comes in a wide variety of weights, materials, and colors, and walking into a yarn store for the first time can feel both exciting and overwhelming. When selecting yarn for an amigurumi project, the main considerations are weight and fiber/material.

YARN WEIGHTS

Yarn weights range from #0 to #7, with #0 (lace) being the thinnest and #7 (jumbo) being the bulkiest. Most amigurumi patterns are made using either worsted/medium weight (#4) yarn or DK/light weight (#3) yarn. Some crocheters also make supersized toys using bulky or jumbo yarn and a large hook. Doing so is an easy way to upsize an existing pattern without changing any stitches.

 Below shows a chart comparing the different yarn weights and corresponding recommended hook sizes. However, for amigurumi you should always select a hook that is one or two sizes lower than stated on the yarn label in order to ensure tight stitches.

STANDARD YARN WEIGHT SYSTEM

YARN WEIGHT SYMBOL AND CATEGORY NAMES	TYPE OF YARNS IN CATEGORY	CROCHET GAUGE* RANGES IN SINGLE CROCHET TO 4 INCHES	RECOMMENDED HOOK IN METRIC SIZE RANGE	RECOMMENDED HOOK U.S. SIZE RANGE
0 Lace	Fingering 10-count crochet thread	32–42 double crochets**	Steel*** 1.6–1.4 mm/Regular hook 2.25 mm	Steel*** 6, 7, 8/Regular hook B-1
1 Super Fine	Sock, Fingering, Baby	21–32 sts	2.25–3.5 mm	B-1 to E-4
2 Fine	Sport, Baby	16–20 sts	3.5–4.5 mm	E-4 to 7

YARN WEIGHT SYMBOL AND CATEGORY NAMES	TYPE OF YARNS IN CATEGORY	CROCHET GAUGE* RANGES IN SINGLE CROCHET TO 4 INCHES	RECOMMENDED HOOK IN METRIC SIZE RANGE	RECOMMENDED HOOK U.S. SIZE RANGE
3 Light	DK, Light Worsted	12–17 sts	4.5–5.5 mm	7 to I-9
4 Medium	Worsted, Afghan, Aran	11–14 sts	5.5–6.5 mm	I-9 to K-10.5
5 Bulky	Chunky, Craft, Rug	8–11 sts	6.5–9 mm	K-10.5 to M-13
6 Super Bulky	Super Bulky, Roving	7–9 sts	9–15 mm	M-13 to Q
7 Jumbo	Jumbo, Roving	6 sts and fewer	15 mm and larger	Q and larger

Source: CraftYarnCouncil.com

* Guidelines only: The gauges in the chart reflect the most commonly used gauges and hook sizes for specific yarn categories.

** Lace weight yarns are usually crocheted on larger hooks to create lacy, openwork patterns. Accordingly, a gauge range is difficult to determine. Always follow the gauge stated in your pattern.

*** Steel crochet hooks are sized differently from regular hooks—the higher the number, the smaller the hook, which is the reverse of regular hook sizing.

YARN MATERIALS

Choosing a yarn material is crucial to the success of your amigurumi project. There are many types of yarn materials, from affordable cotton or acrylic yarns to premium hand-spun and hand-dyed wools. When selecting yarn for your project, consider your budget, the intended recipient, and ease of use.

For example, as beautiful as a skein of hand-dyed alpaca wool may be, I wouldn't recommend it for a child's toy, which needs to hold up through many play sessions, and be both durable and washable. Wool is pricey and difficult to clean, and it may also cause an allergic reaction in people who are sensitive to animal protein fibers.

Most amigurumi are made with either acrylic or cotton yarn, both of which are inexpensive, easy to clean, and available in a wide variety of colors. Acrylic yarn is extremely popular for amigurumi and is my personal material of choice. Acrylic is easy to work with, creates neat and tight stitches, and can be purchased cheaply from any local craft shop.

Cotton yarn is also popular, particularly among eco-conscious crocheters, because it's a natural fiber, whereas acrylic is synthetic and made from plastic. Cotton yarn tends to be stiffer than acrylic and has a clear stitch definition, so the final projects hold their shape well. Cotton is also durable and machine washable, making it a great choice for toys given to young children.

All the projects in this book are made with Bernat® Super Value™ yarn, which is a medium (#4) worsted weight yarn. This acrylic yarn is easy to use, machine washable, and affordable. Bernat Super Value comes in a wide variety of colors and is readily available in local craft stores and online. You can also replace this yarn with another medium (#4) worsted weight yarn.

Accessories

Once you've chosen your hook and yarn, you'll need to gather the following essential supplies:

Pins: A simple set of sewing pins is helpful when you are sewing your amigurumi pieces together. I recommend using large-headed pins that won't slip through the stitches and into your work.

Project bag: Now that you have all these new and exciting tools, you need somewhere to put them. I recommend a zippered pouch—I use a clear pencil case—to hold your day-to-day supplies, and a fabric bag to carry around your current project and yarn. You can also buy specialized project bags for crafting, which include places to store your hooks and notions.

Safety eyes and safety noses: Safety eyes and noses bring your amigurumi to life. They are available in a wide range of sizes, colors, and styles, and are made up of two pieces: the plastic eye or nose piece that shows on the outside, and the washer that snaps over the back. Safety eyes and noses cannot be removed once they are locked in place. You can purchase basic safety eyes and noses in some craft shops, but you'll find the widest variety online. Check out the Resources section for my recommendations.

Scissors: Every crochet tool kit needs a good, sharp pair of scissors. I recommend a small pair with a pointed end that you can easily store and transport.

Stitch markers: Stitch markers are used to mark the beginning of a new round when you crochet. Make sure to purchase a removable stitch marker, ideally one that locks into place so that it can't fall off the piece you are crocheting.

Stuffing: Polyester fiberfill is the most popular option for stuffing your toys and is the material I used to stuff the toys in this book. Fiberfill is lightweight, fluffy, washable, and holds its shape well so your toys don't become lumpy.

Tapestry needle: A tapestry needle (also called a yarn needle or darning needle) is a thick, blunt-tipped needle with an eye that is large enough for yarn. You use tapestry needles to weave in your yarn ends, sew pieces together, and stitch on embellishments.

BONUS TOOLS

As you progress in your amigurumi journey, you may want to add additional tools and materials to your kit that will help you further customize your toys and make them unique. I often use **floral wire** to make my toys posable or to help them hold a certain shape. A good pair of **wire cutters** is necessary if you are adding wire to your toys. Another worthwhile purchase is a bag of **PVC pellets** for weighted stuffing, which can be used to add stability to your toys. Finally, one of the most fun parts of making amigurumi is adding embellishments to give them extra personality, especially if you're making dolls. I always have lots of **craft felt** on hand, along with a good-quality bottle of **craft glue** that I use to add cute details to my dolls.

CARE AND KEEPING OF STUFFED TOYS

Amigurumi toys make wonderful gifts for young children, but you must keep a few things in mind. First, ensure that the toy doesn't pose any safety threats to the child. Safety eyes and noses can be a choking hazard for very young children or pets, and they are not recommended for children under the age of three. Instead, you can embroider yarn eyes and noses onto your toys. You should also avoid adding wire or removable embellishments such as buttons on any toy that will be given to a young child or a pet.

Another important consideration is how to safely wash your amigurumi. After all, children love to play with their toys and get them dirty. First, check the yarn label for care instructions. Some yarns, such as acrylic, are machine washable. Others, such as wool, must be spot cleaned only. For small surface-level stains, you can spot clean your toy with a bit of soapy water and a cloth. Machine washing should be done sparingly to keep your amigurumi looking their best. Always put the toy inside a pillowcase or mesh laundry bag and wash and dry on a delicate cycle.

Reading a Pattern

Crochet patterns may seem overwhelming at first glance, but once you learn the abbreviations and terminology, you will find they are quite straightforward. All crochet patterns are written in a form of shorthand, with standardized abbreviations and terms such as **sc** for single crochet. Amigurumi patterns typically use only a few simple stitches, and they often follow a similar structure of increases and decreases. As you work through the designs in this book, you will become familiar with the basic patterns used to create common shapes such as spheres and cylinders.

Before you start a pattern, always read the information at the beginning, which offers a list of the materials required, the stitches and abbreviations used, and any special notes that will help you complete the pattern. Make sure to gather all the materials and tools listed, including the recommended yarn, hook, and additional supplies.

US vs. UK Abbreviations

Crochet abbreviations and terms vary from country to country, and the most important difference you should note is between the terms used in the United States and the United Kingdom. They use similar terminology, but there is some confusing overlap. For example, a US single crochet is called a double crochet in the United Kingdom, and a double crochet in the United States is called a triple crochet in the United Kingdom. For this book, all the patterns are written in US terms. However, it's good to be aware of both versions in case you come across a pattern written in UK terms. Each crochet pattern will state at the beginning if it uses US or UK terminology.

US TERMS	UK TERMS
chain (ch)	chain (ch)
stitch (**st)**	stitch (**st)**
slip stitch (**sl st)**	slip stitch (**ss)**
single crochet (**sc)**	double crochet (**dc)**
half double crochet (**hdc)**	half treble crochet (**htc)**
double crochet (**dc)**	treble crochet (**tc)**
single crochet decrease (**sc2tog)**	double crochet decrease (**dc2tog)**

Know the Terms

Now that you're familiar with the basic stitch abbreviations, it's time to learn some of the other terminology you'll need to know. Below is a list of common terms, phrases, and concepts you will see in this book's crochet patterns.

Yarn over: The term "yarn over" (abbreviated as **yo** or **yoh**) refers to the act of wrapping the yarn over your crochet hook. Every crochet stitch includes at least one yarn over.

Gauge: Gauge is the measure of how many stitches and rows are created within a specified measurement. When crocheting clothing, you should always crochet a swatch of fabric to ensure that the size of your swatch matches the pattern's gauge. Gauge is less important in amigurumi, but it is important to make sure your tension is sufficiently tight so the stuffing doesn't show through.

Rounds vs. rows: Crochet patterns are worked either in straight rows or in rounds. When working in straight rows, you chain a stitch and turn your work at the end of each row. Most amigurumi are made in the round. You will insert a stitch marker into the first stitch of each round to mark your place. When you reach the end of a round you remove the stitch marker, continue onto the next round without joining or turning, and insert the stitch marker into the first stitch of your new round.

Asterisks and parentheses: Depending on the pattern, either asterisks or parentheses will be used to indicate that a specified section should be repeated a certain number of times. In this book I use asterisks, but you may see parentheses in other patterns. The word "repeat" is abbreviated as **rep**.

Brackets: Square brackets are used to show the final stitch count of each row/round. (Some patterns may use parentheses.)

Yarn tail/end: The tail (or end) of the yarn is the leftover portion when you start a project or fasten off. Always leave a tail of at least 4 or 5 inches so you can weave it in securely.

Basic Crochet Stitches for Amigurumi

In this section, you will find step-by-step illustrated instructions of the basic crochet stitches needed to make amigurumi.

Slip Knot and Chain Stitch (CH)

The chain stitch is the foundational stitch for many crochet projects. When you crochet a flat piece in rows, you normally begin with a foundation chain made up of a specified number of chain stitches. This length of chain stitches is the base onto which you will crochet your first row of stitches. You also always make one chain stitch (**chain 1** or **ch 1**) to turn your work at the end of each row.

You won't use the chain stitch too frequently in this book because amigurumi are made in continuous spirals without turning. However, you may need to use the chain stitch to create flat accessories for your toys such as a scarf.

To make a foundation chain, you first create a slip knot on your hook.

How to make a slip knot:

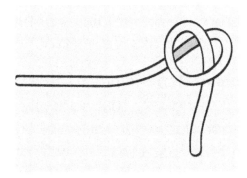

Step 1: Take a few inches of the working yarn and form a loop with your fingers. Lay the loop over the working yarn.

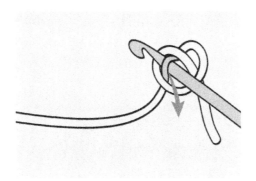

Step 2: Insert your hook through the center of the loop you just made, and grab the working end of the yarn.

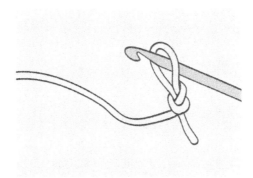

Step 3: Pull the yarn you've grabbed through the center of the loop, then hold on to the tail end firmly and pull the crochet hook up to tighten the knot.

How to make a chain stitch:

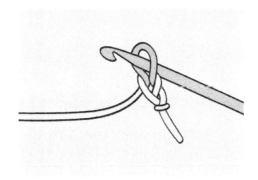

Step 1: Once you have a slip knot, hold the hook in your right hand and the base of the slip knot with the thumb and ring finger of your left hand, with

the strand of working yarn positioned between your index and middle fingers.

Step 2: With the hook still in your right hand, yarn over and pull the yarn through the loop on the hook. (Do not pull this loop too tight; you want to be able to insert the hook into this stitch later.)

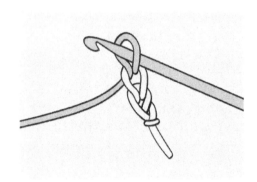

Step 3: Continue to yarn over and pull the yarn through the loop on the hook until you create the required number of chain stitches. Never count the loop on the hook or the starting slip knot as stitches. Practice working a chain stitch, then practice it some more until you are comfortable managing the hook and yarn and the chains are consistent in size.

Slip Stitch (SL ST)

The slip stitch is a simple stitch typically used to join sections or to finish off a section. This stitch doesn't add much height to your work, so it is also useful for adding embellishments.

How to make a slip stitch:

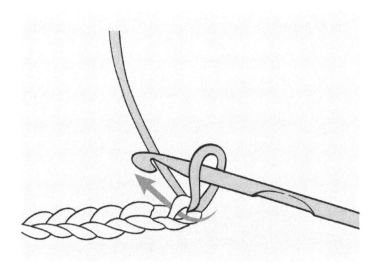

Step 1: Insert the hook into the stitch indicated in the pattern.

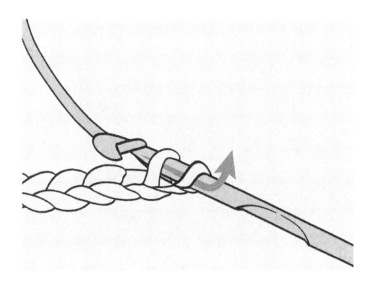

Step 2: Yarn over and pull the hook through the stitch and the loop on the hook at the same time.

Single Crochet (SC)

The single crochet is an essential stitch to master, and fortunately, it's also one of the easiest. This basic stitch is the building block of crochet, and most other stitches are variations on the single crochet. The majority of amigurumi are made using the single crochet because it creates a tight, stiff fabric that hides the stuffing in your toys. Therefore, it's definitely worth taking the time to practice and become comfortable with single crochet.

How to make a single crochet:

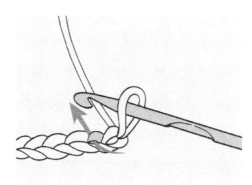

Step 1: Insert your hook into the next stitch and yarn over.

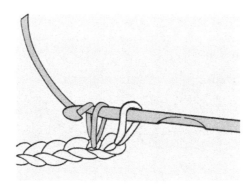

Step 2: Pull the hook through the stitch only (2 loops on the hook).

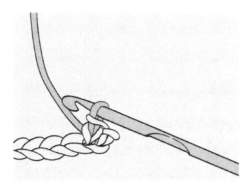

Step 3: Yarn over and pull the hook through the remaining two loops on the hook.

Half Double Crochet (HDC)

The half double crochet is a taller stitch than the single crochet, but not quite as tall as the double crochet. It's a great option you can use to add more height to your work, and it creates a looser fabric than the single crochet.

How to make a half double crochet:

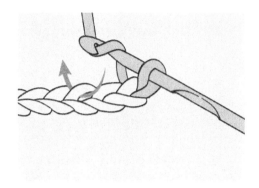

Step 1: Yarn over and insert the hook into the indicated stitch.

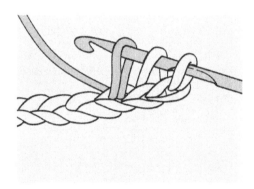

Step 2: Yarn over and pull the hook through the stitch (3 loops on the hook).

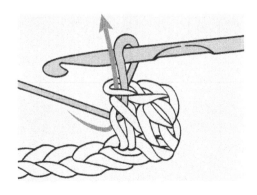

Step 3: Yarn over and pull the hook through all three loops on the hook.

Double Crochet (DC)

The double crochet is twice as tall as the single crochet and is a popular stitch for garments, hats, and scarves. You won't see double crochet used very often in amigurumi; however, there are times when you may use it for shaping and to create doll accessories.

How to make a double crochet:

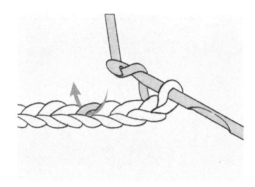

Step 1: Yarn over and insert the hook into the indicated stitch.

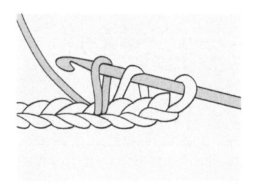

Step 2: Yarn over and pull the hook through the stitch (3 loops on the hook).

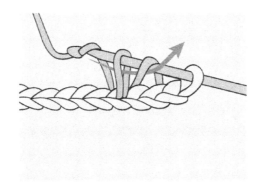

Step 3: Yarn over and pull the hook through only the first two loops on the hook (2 loops on the hook).

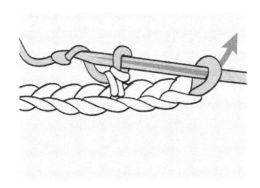

Step 4: Yarn over and pull the hook through the last two loops on the hook.

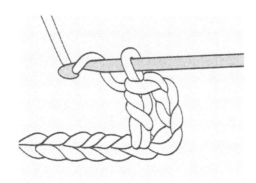

Step 5: Finished double crochet stitch with turning chain.

Magic Ring/Circle

The magic ring (or magic circle) is a crucial skill used to start a project in the round. The magic ring creates a tightly closed center with no visible hole in the middle.

How to make a magic ring:

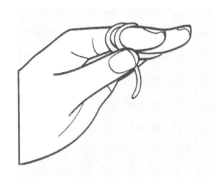

Step 1: With the tail end closest to you, drape the working end of the yarn over your left-hand index and third fingers. Wrap the working end around both fingers one time.

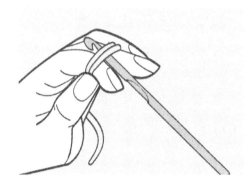

Step 2: Insert the hook between the yarn and the top of your fingers. With your right-hand index finger and thumb, hold the yarn in place and drop the left hand from the ring.

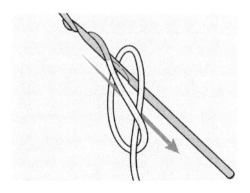

Step 3: With your left hand, secure the working end of the yarn. Hook the working yarn and pull it through the center of the ring.

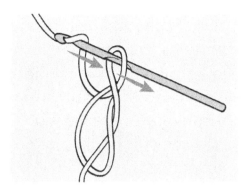

Step 4: Chain one to secure the ring.

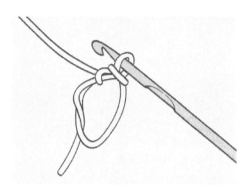

Step 5: You work into the magic ring by crocheting through the center of the ring.

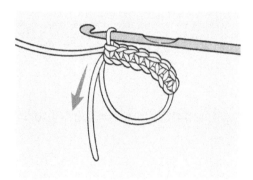

Step 6: When you have the desired number of stitches, gently pull the tail tight to cinch the ring closed.

Increasing and Decreasing (INC and DEC)

Increasing and decreasing are where the magic happens in amigurumi. You will use these two techniques to create three-dimensional shapes such as spheres, cylinders, and cones.

An increase is simply two stitches made into the same stitch. In this book, increases are written using the abbreviation **inc**. Other patterns may use the phrase "make 2 sc in next st" or something similar. By making an increase, you are adding an additional stitch to your round.

A decrease is the opposite of an increase: You crochet two existing stitches together to remove one stitch from your round. The abbreviation **dec** is used to designate a decrease in this book, but you will also see "sc2tog" in other patterns.

How to make an increase:

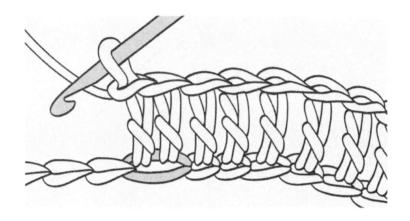

To increase, make 2 stitches in the same space to increase the row count by 1. For instance, the illustration here shows two double crochets made into the same stitch, to increase by one.

How to make a single crochet decrease:

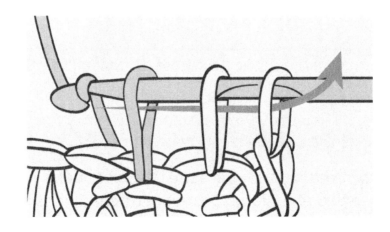

Step 1: Insert the hook into the indicated stitch, yarn over, and pull the hook through the stitch (2 loops on the hook). Instead of finishing the stitch, leave those two loops where they are. Insert the hook into the next stitch, yarn over and pull the hook through the stitch (3 loops on the hook).

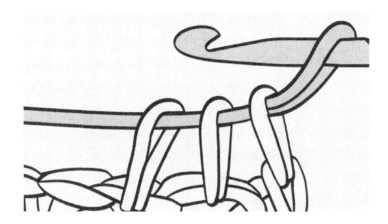

Step 2: Now, combine the two stitches you've just made by finishing them all off at the same time: Yarn over and pull the hook through all three loops on the hook.

Crocheting in the Back Loop or Front Loop Only (BLO and FLO)

Normally when you crochet, you work under both loops at the top of a stitch. However, there are times when a pattern will instruct you to work under the back loop only (**BLO**) or the front loop only (**FLO**). By working under only one loop, you create a ridge made up of the unused loops. This ridge may be decorative, or it can be used as a base on which to crochet additional details. When you crochet in the back loop only around the entire round, there will be a ridge of the leftover front loops on the outside of your work. When you crochet in the front loop only around the entire round, there will be a ridge of the leftover back loops on the inside of your work.

Counting Stitches and Rounds

Miscounting your stitches or rounds is a common challenge for beginner crocheters. A missed stitch or round can alter the shape and size of your amigurumi, so it's important to follow the pattern instructions carefully and check your stitch count regularly.

Not sure how to count your stitches? The top of each stitch resembles a V shape, with two loops (front and back). You count the number of V shapes to know how many stitches you've made in a row or round. Do not count the loop that is on your hook (Figure 1.1, <u>Fergus the Fun-Loving Fox</u>).

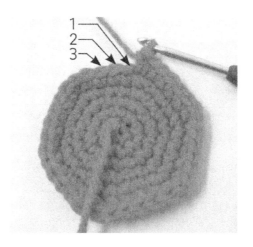

Figure 1.1: How to count stitches

Throughout the patterns in this book, I refer to specific rounds for the placement of limbs and safety eyes. For example, I may instruct you to insert the safety eyes "between Rounds 10 and 11." Counting rounds is quite simple. The first round is the small circle of stitches in the middle of the piece, where you made your magic ring. The subsequent rounds are the ridges you can see in Figure 1.2, from <u>Fergus the Fun-Loving Fox</u>.

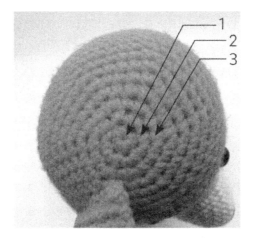

Figure 1.2: How to count rounds

Front vs. Back of Crochet Fabric

When you crochet in a continuous spiral without turning your work, you will notice that the front and back side of the stitches look quite different. Amigurumi are typically made with the front side of the stitches (also known as the right side or RS) showing because most people prefer how front stitches look compared to back stitches (also called the wrong side or WS).

When you are crocheting in the round, your work will naturally start to curve into a bowl shape, with the back side of the stitches showing to the outside (Figure 1.3, Fergus the Fun-Loving Fox). To fix this, flip your work inside out after a few rounds. Now the front side of the stitches will be on the outside of the bowl and you will be crocheting around the outer rim of the bowl by inserting your hook from outside to inside and working in a clockwise direction (Figure 1.4).

Figure 1.3: The back stitches are on the outside

Figure 1.4: The front stitches are now on the outside

Sample Pattern Line

Now that you understand the terms and abbreviations, let's put it all together. Here is a sample line from a pattern in this book:

Round 4: *Sc 2, inc; rep from * 5 more times. [24 sts]

To complete Round 4, you single crochet in the first two stitches and then increase in the third stitch. You will repeat these instructions a total of six times around. The "24 sts" in brackets indicates that you will have 24 stitches when you finish the round.

COLOR CHANGES

Several of the patterns in this book will instruct you to change yarn colors partway through a piece. Changing colors allows you to create effects such as stripes and color patches. Fortunately, creating color changes is really easy. Simply work the last stitch before the color change as normal until the step before your final yarn over. Instead of pulling your current color through the loops on your hook, drop the old color to the back of your work and yarn over with the new color. Complete the stitch with the new color, and you've done it.

You can use a few different methods to secure your yarn tails from a color change. If you are making an amigurumi piece that will be closed up and stuffed, such as a head, then you can tie the ends into a knot inside the piece. However, if the back side of the piece will be visible, then you will need to weave in the ends of the yarn to secure and hide them. If you will be using the old color again in a couple of stitches or rows, to make stripes, for example, then you can carry the yarn along the inside and pick it up again as needed. This technique should only be used if there is a small gap between two areas with the same color.

Assembly and Finishing

Once you've completed the individual pieces for your amigurumi, it's time to put it all together. Sewing amigurumi together can be tricky, but your hard work will pay off when you see your toy take shape and come to life. In this section, I'll go over the different techniques you'll need to assemble and finish your amigurumi, including stuffing, joining pieces, and adding details.

Fastening Off and Closing Up

At the end of each piece within a pattern, you might see the phrase "finish off" or "fasten off," sometimes abbreviated as **FO**. You may be tempted to just tie a knot and cut the yarn but resist that urge. Properly weaving in your yarn ends takes a few more minutes, but it's worth it to avoid unsightly knots and to prevent your work from unraveling.

Fastening off an open piece:

An open piece is left open at the top and then sewn onto the main piece. For example, arms, legs, and snouts are all open pieces.

Step 1: Slip stitch into the next stitch.

Step 2: Cut the yarn, leaving a yarn tail of at least 8 to 10 inches so you can sew your pieces together.

Step 3: Pull the hook upward to draw the yarn tail through the slip stitch, and tighten the knot (Figure 1.5).

Figure 1.5: Draw the yarn tail up through the slip stitch to fasten off (as shown in <u>Sofia the Sleepy Sloth</u>)

Closing up a 3D flattened piece:

A 3D flattened piece is worked in the round as a 3D piece and is then flattened without being stuffed. This technique is used throughout the book to make body parts such as ears, wings, and flippers. Some stuffed pieces are also flattened at the open end, such as the tops of arms. The following come from the ears of <u>Fergus the Fun-Loving Fox</u>.

Figure 1.6: Flatten the piece

Step 1: Once you complete the final round of the piece, follow the steps in "Fastening off an open piece" to finish off the open piece.

Figure 1.7: Sew the front and back edges together

Step 2: Press the open edges together to flatten the piece. The edges should be flush against each other, with the final stitch off to the side (Figure 1.6).

Figure 1.8: Completed flattened piece

Step 3: Sew the front and back edges together using a whip stitch, working straight across the opening and inserting your needle under both loops of two stitches (Figures 1.7 and 1.8).

Closing up a closed piece:

When making a closed piece, such as a ball, you will need to close up the remaining hole with a tapestry needle.

Step 1: After the final round, cut the yarn, draw through the last loop on your hook, and pull to tighten. Leave a tail that's at least 5 inches long.

Step 2: Thread the yarn onto your tapestry needle.

Step 3: Insert your needle under the front loop of the next stitch, pull tight, and continue weaving through the remaining stitches until the hole is closed, as shown in <u>Fergus the Fun-Loving Fox</u> (Figure 1.9).

Figure 1.9: Sewing the hole closed

Step 4: Insert your needle through the middle of the closed hole and run the yarn through the piece to hide it (Figure 1.10).

Figure 1.10: Hiding the yarn tail

Hiding and weaving in yarn ends:

Once you've finished sewing your pieces together, you will need to hide your yarn ends. For a closed and stuffed piece, this is easy. Thread the yarn onto your needle, insert it into the piece, and bring the needle up a few inches away. Pull the yarn up a bit, cut it, and the end will vanish back into the piece. Make sure the yarn end is still 2 to 3 inches long when you do this and insert it far into your piece, as shown in <u>Sofia the Sleepy Sloth</u> (Figure 1.11).

Figure 1.11: Hiding ends in a closed piece

For an open piece where the ends cannot be hidden, you will need to weave them in. Thread your needle with the yarn end, and then weave the yarn through your stitches for an inch or two. Go back and forth a couple of times to ensure the end is secure, and then cut the yarn (Figure 1.12 from <u>Fergus's belly</u>).

Figure 1.12: Weaving in ends in an open piece

Stuffing

Stuffing is one of my favorite parts of assembling amigurumi, because it's when the pieces I've crocheted start to take shape. There are a few important tips and tricks you need to consider. First, make sure that your stuffing is light and airy, and not clumped together into a ball (Figure 1.13, from <u>Sofia the Sleepy Sloth</u>). Clumped-up stuffing will make your toys look lumpy and misshapen. Gently pull apart the stuffing to fluff it up, and then insert small amounts at a time. Push the stuffing to the bottom of the piece before you add more. Do not reuse stuffing that has become bunched up.

Figure 1.13: It's always best to use new, fluffy stuffing

Second, be sure to stuff firmly. Too little stuffing will make your amigurumi floppy and unable to sit up properly. Stuffing tends to settle with time, so your amigurumi will naturally get softer over the years. You should always stuff the neck area so that it's particularly firm because it must be able to hold up the head. You can stuff other areas more lightly, such as the tops of arms and legs, to ensure that they sit well against the body (Figure 1.14).

Figure 1.14: Ensure pieces are stuffed firmly so they hold their shape

Finally, I recommend stuffing thinner pieces such as arms and legs as you work. Once you're about 8 to 10 rounds in, begin adding some stuffing. Continue to add stuffing every few rounds. You can use a thin wooden dowel or chopstick to help you stuff small and tight spaces. Keep adding more stuffing as you reach the end, and you can even add a bit more stuffing when you are closing up the piece or sewing it to the body (Figure 1.15).

Figure 1.15: Adding extra stuffing as you sew pieces together

Placement

Before you sew any pieces together, take the time to ensure everything is placed the way you want it. For a polished and professional finish, you want your amigurumi to be as symmetrical as possible. With that said, remember that each amigurumi is unique and handmade, so if something is a bit off, it'll just give your toy extra personality.

My number one piece of advice is to use pins—lots of pins. I recommend pinning all the parts of your amigurumi together before you start sewing. Look at your toy from all angles once it's pinned together. Are the arms symmetrical? Are the ears placed evenly on either side of the head? Make sure you are happy with how everything looks, because it's challenging to remove pieces once they're sewn on.

Crochet rounds and stitches provide a handy guide for placing your amigurumi pieces. For example, when you are sewing on arms, you should always line up the top of the arm so it lies straight along the stitches of the body (Figure 1.16 from Sofia the Sleepy Sloth). Follow that round to the other side of the body and pin the second arm to match the first.

Figure 1.16: Ensure the arm is straight and the "hand" is curved inward

Where you place the legs is particularly important for sitting toys. Like the arms, the tops of the legs should be evenly lined up to the same round. Position the legs several rounds up from the bottom of the body so they stick out in front. Pin the legs in place, and then check that your toy sits up properly. If it falls backward, move the legs up a couple of rounds (Figure 1.17).

Figure 1.17: Make sure the "foot" is pointing upward when you sew on the leg

Finally, you'll want to consider the position of color changes when you're assembling your amigurumi. You'll notice that color changes create a "jog" at the spot where you changed colors. Whenever possible, arrange your amigurumi so this jog is covered by another piece or is angled toward the back.

Joining Parts

You've stuffed all your pieces and pinned them in place. Now you're ready to start sewing. Many amigurumi makers dislike this part of the process because it can be time-consuming and fussy. Personally, I love seeing my amigurumi come together. Watching my creation go from a bunch of individual body pieces to a completed animal or doll is so satisfying. With a bit of practice, you will soon get the hang of sewing amigurumi pieces together.

First, remember all the pinning you just did? Keep those pins in. You may want to remove some pieces so they don't get in the way when you're sewing, but I recommend marking the placement of those pieces with pins or stitch markers so you remember where to put them back. However, keep the piece you're sewing pinned so it doesn't move around while you sew it down. Here's an example from Sofia the Sleepy Sloth:

Joining pieces together:

Step 1: Make sure you left a long yarn tail when you fastened off. If you forgot and cut it too short, don't worry. You can cut a new length of longer yarn and use that to sew your pieces together.

Step 2: Thread your tapestry needle with the yarn tail.

Step 3: Insert the needle into the main piece, just below the first stitch on the piece you are joining (Figure 1.18). Pull the yarn through firmly, but not so tightly that it warps the shape.

Figure 1.18

Step 4: Bring the needle back through the next stitch on the piece you are joining and pull the yarn through (Figure 1.19). Continue working through each stitch around your piece until you get back to the first stitch. You can also add more stuffing as you go.

Figure 1.19

When joining a flattened piece to your animal, for example an ear or wing, make sure to sew along both the front and back sides of the piece. First, work down one side of the piece, inserting your needle into the loops at the base on that side (Figure 1.20, from <u>Fergus the Fun-Loving Fox</u>). When you get to the opposite edge, continue around to the other side and sew back across to your starting point (Figure 1.21). This will ensure that your piece is secured on both sides and will not flop around.

Figure 1.20: Sew along one side of the ear

Figure 1.21: Next, sew along the other side of the ear

Figure 1.22: Ear completely sewn on

Face and Body Details

Once you've added the face and details, your amigurumi's personality will really shine through. Simple touches like embroidered eyebrows or a mouth can make an amigurumi look happy, sad, angry, or surprised.

Safety eyes and safety noses are both easy to use and will give your projects a polished and professional look. You will add safety eyes and noses to your project once you're partway through the head, and before you stuff it. The patterns in this book all provide instructions for when to add the eyes and nose and which rounds to place them between.

Once the eyes and nose are in place, you can embroider on any additional details, such as mouths or whiskers. I typically add these details after the amigurumi is stuffed and closed up, so I can see exactly how they will look. You can embroider on these features using yarn, or for smaller details you can use embroidery thread. Use your crochet stitches as a guide for the placement of each embroidered stitch and go slowly.

Finally, it's okay if you have to take your work out and redo it a few times to get the exact look you want. Embroidering details onto crochet is tricky. Keep practicing.

PART 2

PATTERN PROJECTS

The twenty amigurumi patterns featured in this book are organized from simple to slightly more challenging (but still easy) projects. In the first few projects, you focus on developing basic skills, such as creating spheres, sewing on flattened pieces, and practicing color changes. If you are new to amigurumi, I recommend starting with one of the first four patterns. All the patterns are beginner-friendly so that once you've made a couple of animals, you shouldn't have trouble making the rest. A few patterns use special techniques to create unique pieces, such as the orca tail or the raccoon and sloth eyes. Photo tutorials are included to help you master these more complex skills.

All the pattern pieces in this book are made in a continuous spiral, unless otherwise noted. Mark the first stitch of each round with a stitch marker, and do not join rounds or turn at the end of each round.

BUILD A BEAR (OR ANYTHING ELSE)

This book may be your first foray into making amigurumi, but there is a whole huge world of patterns and ideas out there to inspire you. The projects in this book will provide you with foundational skills such as increasing, decreasing, changing colors, and assembling your finished toys. All amigurumi patterns are built on these skills, and even the most complex-looking designs are often made using the simplest stitches and techniques.

Many of the animals in this book share the same or similar body and limb patterns. For example, the raccoon, bunny, frog, and cat are based on the same basic pattern. Likewise, the five large animals (monkey, sloth, panda, koala, and fox) all have the same head, body, and limbs. Simply adding extra details like snouts and ears gives each animal its individual shape and personality. Even just changing colors can give you a whole new animal. For example, the panda pattern in all white yarn would become a polar bear, or the fox pattern with gray and white yarn would become a wolf.

Once you've completed a few patterns and gotten the hang of how to make the different shapes, you can start to mix and match them to create your own characters. Perhaps you want a larger cat. You could make the fox pattern in your preferred cat colors but leave off the snout and tail. Then, add more stitches and rounds to the cat tail pattern to make it bigger. Or you could combine the raccoon body and snout patterns with the dachshund ear and tail patterns to make a sitting dog. There are so many possibilities.

NELLIE THE NERVOUS OCTOPUS

Nellie is a gentle but nervous octopus who lives among the coral reefs of Australia. She is always ready to help a diver in need, but at the first sign of danger she tends to run away and change color to disguise herself. Nellie is a great beginner amigurumi project. She is very simple to make and will give you lots of practice crocheting spheres and sewing them together.

Size: 3½ inches high

MATERIALS:

Bernat Super Value medium 4 (100% acrylic; 426 yards (389 m)/197 g): Light Damson, 125 yards

US size G-6 (4.00 mm) crochet hook

2 (12-mm) black safety eyes

Polyester fiberfill

Tapestry needle

Removable stitch marker

STITCHES USED:

Magic ring

Single crochet (sc)

Increase (inc)

Decrease (dec)

BODY:

Using Light Damson yarn:

Round 1: Sc 6 in a magic ring. [6 sts]

Round 2: Inc around. [12 sts]

Round 3: *Sc, inc; rep from * 5 more times. [18 sts]

Round 4: *Sc 2, inc; rep from * 5 more times. [24 sts]

Round 5: *Sc 3, inc; rep from * 5 more times. [30 sts]

Round 6: *Sc 4, inc; rep from * 5 more times. [36 sts]

Round 7: *Sc 5, inc; rep from * 5 more times. [42 sts]

Round 8: *Sc 6, inc; rep from * 5 more times. [48 sts]

Rounds 9–18: Sc around. [48 sts]

Round 19: *Sc 6, dec; rep from * 5 more times. [42 sts]

Round 20: *Sc 5, dec; rep from * 5 more times. [36 sts]

Round 21: *Sc 4, dec; rep from * 5 more times. [30 sts]

Insert the safety eyes between Rounds 10 and 11, about six stitches apart. Begin stuffing the body and continue to add stuffing as you crochet the remaining rounds.

Round 22: *Sc 3, dec; rep from * 5 more times. [24 sts]

Round 23: *Sc 2, dec; rep from * 5 more times. [18 sts]

Round 24: *Sc, dec; rep from * 5 more times. [12 sts]

Round 25: Dec around. [6 sts]

Finish off and close up the hole.

TENTACLES (MAKE 8):

Using Light Damson yarn:

Round 1: Sc 6 in a magic ring. [6 sts]

Round 2: Inc around. [12 sts]

Round 3: *Sc, inc; rep from * 5 more times. [18 sts]

Rounds 4–8: Sc around. [18 sts]

Round 9: *Sc 4, dec; rep from * 2 more times. [15 sts]

Round 10: Sc around. [15 sts]

Finish off, leaving a long end. Stuff each tentacle and sew them evenly around the bottom of the body, under Round 16. I recommend pinning all eight tentacles to the body before you sew any of them down, to ensure that the placement is correct and that none of the gaps between the tentacles are too large or small.

SIGRID THE SINGING SEAL

Sigrid spends her days playing in the icy waters of her Icelandic lagoon and dreaming of becoming an opera singer. When sailors pass by, she always serenades them with a song. As she listens to the sound of their cheers and applause, she closes her eyes and imagines herself on the stage of the famous Harpa Concert Hall in Reykjavik.

In this pattern, you will practice crocheting 3D pieces that you then flatten to make appendages such as wings, ears, and flippers. Refer here for instructions on how to assemble flattened pieces.

Size: 7½ inches long, 3½ inches high

MATERIALS:
Bernat Super Value medium 4 (100% acrylic; 426 yards (389 m)/197 g): True Gray, 90 yards
White, 10 yards
US size G-6 (4.00 mm) crochet hook
2 (12-mm) black safety eyes
1 (15-mm) black safety nose
Polyester fiberfill
Tapestry needle
Removable stitch marker

STITCHES USED:
Magic ring
Single crochet (sc)
Increase (inc)
Decrease (dec)

BODY:

Using True Gray yarn:

Round 1: Sc 6 in a magic ring. [6 sts]

Round 2: Inc around. [12 sts]

Round 3: *Sc, inc; rep from * 5 more times. [18 sts]

Round 4: *Sc 2, inc; rep from * 5 more times. [24 sts]

Round 5: *Sc 3, inc; rep from * 5 more times. [30 sts]

Round 6: *Sc 4, inc; rep from * 5 more times. [36 sts]

Round 7: *Sc 5, inc; rep from * 5 more times. [42 sts]

Round 8: *Sc 6, inc; rep from * 5 more times. [48 sts]

Rounds 9–20: Sc around. [48 sts]

Insert the safety eyes at the front of the seal between Rounds 5 and 6, about eight stitches apart.

Round 21: *Sc 6, dec; rep from * 5 more times. [42 sts]

Round 22: Sc around. [42 sts]

Round 23: *Sc 5, dec; rep from * 5 more times. [36 sts]

Round 24: Sc around. [36 sts]

Round 25: *Sc 4, dec; rep from * 5 more times. [30 sts]

Round 26: Sc around. [30 sts]

Begin stuffing the body and continue to add stuffing as you crochet the remaining rounds.

Round 27: *Sc 3, dec; rep from * 5 more times. [24 sts]

Round 28: Sc around. [24 sts]

Round 29: *Sc 2, dec; rep from * 5 more times. [18 sts]

Round 30: *Sc, dec; rep from * 5 more times. [12 sts]

Round 31: Dec around. [6 sts]

Finish off and close up the hole.

SNOUT:

Using White yarn:

Round 1: Sc 6 in a magic ring. [6 sts]

Round 2: Inc around. [12 sts]

Round 3: *Sc, inc; rep from * 5 more times. [18 sts]

Round 4: *Sc 5, inc; rep from * 2 more times. [21 sts]

Rounds 5–6: Sc around. [21 sts]

Finish off, leaving a long end. Insert the safety nose between Rounds 1 and 2. The flat part of the nose should be facing up, and the bottom of the nose should be pointing down to the middle hole from Round 1. Stuff the snout, then sew it to the face, between the eyes. Continue to add more stuffing to the snout as you sew it on.

SIDE FLIPPERS (MAKE 2):

Using True Gray yarn:

Round 1: Sc 6 in a magic ring. [6 sts]

Round 2: Inc around. [12 sts]

Round 3: *Sc, inc; rep from * 5 more times. [18 sts]

Rounds 4–5: Sc around. [18 sts]

Round 6: *Sc 4, dec; rep from * 2 more times. [15 sts]

Round 7: Sc around. [15 sts]

Round 8: *Sc 3, dec; rep from * 2 more times. [12 sts]

Round 9: Sc around. [12 sts]

Round 10: *Sc 2, dec; rep from * 2 more times. [9 sts]

Finish off, leaving a long end. Do not stuff. Instead, press the open edges together to flatten the flipper, and then sew straight across the opening to close it up. Sew the flippers toward the front side of the body, about an inch below and behind the eyes.

TAIL FLIPPERS (MAKE 2):

Using True Gray yarn:

Round 1: Sc 6 in a magic ring. [6 sts]

Round 2: Inc around. [12 sts]

Rounds 3–4: Sc around. [12 sts]

Round 5: *Sc 2, dec; rep from * 2 more times. [9 sts]

Round 6: Sc around. [sts]

Round 7: *Sc, dec; rep from * 2 more times. [6 sts]

Finish off, leaving a long end. Do not stuff. Instead, press the open edges together to flatten the flipper, and then sew straight across the opening to close it up. Sew the flippers to the tail end of the body, positioned next to each other.

BEATRICE THE BUMBLING BEE

Beatrice works hard to gather nectar for her busy hive in rural England, but she's not the most coordinated bee. In spite of her bumbling nature, though, she never gives up and always tries her best to support her fellow bees and her queen. This is a quick and easy project to practice your color-changing skills. Check out the Color Changes section if you need a refresher.

Size: 5½ inches long, 5 inches high

MATERIALS:
Bernat Super Value medium 4 (100% acrylic; 426 yards (389 m)/197 g): Bright Yellow, 48 yards
Black, 40 yards
White, 20 yards
US size G-6 (4.00 mm) crochet hook
2 (12-mm) black safety eyes
Polyester fiberfill
Tapestry needle
Removable stitch marker

STITCHES USED:
Magic ring
Single crochet (sc)
Increase (inc)
Decrease (dec)

BODY:

Using Bright Yellow yarn:

Round 1: Sc 6 in a magic ring. [6 sts]

Round 2: Inc around. [12 sts]

Round 3: *Sc, inc; rep from * 5 more times. [18 sts]

Round 4: *Sc 2, inc; rep from * 5 more times. [24 sts]

Round 5: *Sc 3, inc; rep from * 5 more times. [30 sts]

Round 6: *Sc 4, inc; rep from * 5 more times. [36 sts]

Round 7: *Sc 5, inc; rep from * 5 more times. [42 sts]

Round 8: *Sc 6, inc; rep from * 5 more times. [48 sts]

Rounds 9–13: Sc around. [48 sts]

Insert the safety eyes at the front of the bee between Rounds 5 and 6, about nine stitches apart.

Switch to Black yarn:

Rounds 14–16: Sc around. [48 sts]

Switch to Bright Yellow yarn:

Rounds 17–19: Sc around. [48 sts]

Switch to Black yarn:

Rounds 20–22: Sc around. [48 sts]

Switch to Bright Yellow yarn:

Rounds 23–25: Sc around. [48 sts]

Switch to Black yarn:

Round 26: *Sc 6, dec; rep from * 5 more times. [42 sts]

Round 27: *Sc 5, dec; rep from * 5 more times. [36 sts]

Round 28: *Sc 4, dec; rep from * 5 more times. [30 sts]

Begin stuffing the body and continue to add stuffing as you crochet the remaining rounds.

Round 29: *Sc 3, dec; rep from * 5 more times. [24 sts]

Round 30: *Sc 2, dec; rep from * 5 more times. [18 sts]

Round 31: *Sc, dec; rep from * 5 more times. [12 sts]

Round 32: Dec around. [6 sts]

Finish off and close up the hole.

WINGS (MAKE 2):

Using White yarn:

Round 1: Sc 6 in a magic ring. [6 sts]

Round 2: Inc around. [12 sts]

Round 3: *Sc, inc; rep from * 5 more times. [18 sts]

Rounds 4–8: Sc around. [18 sts]

Round 9: *Sc, dec; rep from * 5 more times. [12 sts]

Round 10: Dec around. [6 sts]

Finish off, leaving a long end. Do not stuff. Instead, press the open edges together to flatten the wing, and then sew straight across the opening to close it up. Sew the wings directly next to each other at the top-middle of the bee, making sure they are centered between the eyes.

ANTENNAE (MAKE 2):

Using Black yarn:

Round 1: Sc 6 in a magic ring. [6 sts]

Round 2: Inc around. [12 sts]

Rounds 3–5: Sc around. [12 sts]

Round 6: *Sc, dec; rep from * 3 more times. [8 sts]

Stuff the tips of the antennae and continue to add stuffing as you crochet the remaining rounds.

Rounds 7–11: Sc around. [8 sts]

Finish off, leaving a long end. Sew the antennae to the bee, just above Round 8. They should be about eight stitches apart, and evenly placed over the eyes.

SANTIAGO THE SHY SNAKE

Santiago may look scary, but he's really a very shy snake. Tourists visit his jungle home in Brazil hoping for a glimpse of his colorful stripes, but they end up disappointed because he always hides until they leave. Don't be intimidated by all the color changes. By the time you finish this project, you'll be a pro.

Size: 42 inches long

MATERIALS:

Bernat Super Value medium 4 (100% acrylic; 426 yards (389 m)/197 g): Lush, 140 yards

Hot Blue, 110 yards

Berry, 1 yard

US size G-6 (4.00 mm) crochet hook

2 (12-mm) black safety eyes

Polyester fiberfill

Tapestry needle

Removable stitch marker

STITCHES USED:

Magic ring

Chain (ch)

Single crochet (sc)

Increase (inc)

Decrease (dec)

HEAD AND BODY:

Using Lush yarn:

Round 1: Sc 6 in a magic ring. [6 sts]

Round 2: Inc around. [12 sts]

Round 3: *Sc, inc; rep from * 5 more times. [18 sts]

Round 4: Sc around. [18 sts]

Round 5: *Sc 2, inc; rep from * 5 more times. [24 sts]

Round 6: Sc around. [24 sts]

Round 7: *Sc 3, inc; rep from * 5 more times. [30 sts]

Round 8: Sc around. [30 sts]

Round 9: *Sc 4, inc; rep from * 5 more times. [36 sts]

Round 10: Sc around. [36 sts]

Round 11: *Sc 5, inc; rep from * 5 more times. [42 sts]

Rounds 12–16: Sc around. [42 sts]

Round 17: *Sc 5, dec; rep from * 5 more times. [36 sts]

Round 18: *Sc 4, dec; rep from * 5 more times. [30 sts]

Round 19: *Sc 3, dec; rep from * 5 more times. [24 sts]

Round 20–22: Sc around. [24 sts]

Insert the safety eyes between Rounds 10 and 11, about eight stitches apart. Stuff the head firmly. Continue to stuff every eight to ten rounds as you make the body. The snake's stripes are too wide to carry your yarn, so you will need to cut the yarn after each color change. Make sure to knot the ends inside your snake as you go.

Switch to Hot Blue yarn:

Rounds 23–30: Sc around. [24 sts]

Switch to Lush yarn:

Rounds 31–38: Sc around. [24 sts]

Rounds 39–134: Repeat Rounds 23 to 38 another six times until you have a total of seven blue stripes and seven green stripes. Once you complete the final row of the seventh green stripe (Round 134) you will switch back to blue and begin decreasing to taper the snake off.

Using Hot Blue yarn:

Round 135: *Sc 10, dec; rep from * 1 more time. [22 sts]
Rounds 136–142: Sc around. [22 sts]

Switch to Lush yarn:

Round 143: *Sc 9, dec; rep from * 1 more time. [20 sts]
Rounds 144–150: Sc around. [20 sts]

Switch to Hot Blue yarn:

Round 151: *Sc 8, dec; rep from * 1 more time. [18 sts]
Rounds 152–158: Sc around. [18 sts]

Switch to Lush yarn:

Round 159: *Sc 7, dec; rep from * 1 more time. [16 sts]
Rounds 160–166: Sc around. [16 sts]

Switch to Hot Blue yarn:

Round 167: *Sc 6, dec; rep from * 1 more time. [14 sts]
Rounds 168–174: Sc around. [14 sts]

Switch to Lush yarn:

Round 175: *Sc 5, dec; rep from * 1 more time. [12 sts]
Rounds 176–182: Sc around. [12 sts]

Switch to Hot Blue yarn:

Round 183: *Sc 4, dec; rep from * 1 more time. [10 sts]
Rounds 184–190: Sc around. [10 sts]

Switch to Lush yarn:

Round 191: *Sc 3, dec; rep from * 1 more time. [8 sts]

Rounds 192–198: Sc around. [8 sts]

Round 199: Dec around. [4 sts]

Finish off and close up the hole.

TONGUE:

Using Berry yarn:

Ch 11, then sc in second ch from hook and in next two chains. Ch 4, then sc in second Ch from hook and in next two chains. This will create the forked tongue. Continue down the original chain: Sc 7 in remaining chains. Finish off and sew the tongue to the snake at the middle hole from Round 1.

OLYMPIA THE OFFBEAT OWL

Olympia aspires to be as wise and mysterious as her fellow owls, but the truth is she isn't very good at it. The last time she tried to sit on a branch in the dark and intimidate passing travelers, she fell off. Olympia doesn't mind being different, though, and she enjoys flying around the forests of Greece with her friends. In this simple round owl pattern, you will learn to make a variety of common amigurumi shapes, including flat eye patches and triangular pieces.

Size: 3½ inches high

MATERIALS:

Bernat Super Value medium 4 (100% acrylic; 426 yards (389 m)/197 g): Taupe, 90 yards

Bright Yellow, 6 yards

Carrot, 6 yards

US size G-6 (4.00 mm) crochet hook

2 (12-mm) black safety eyes

Polyester fiberfill

Tapestry needle

Removable stitch marker

STITCHES USED:

Magic ring

Single crochet (sc)

Increase (inc)

Decrease (dec)

BODY:

Using Taupe yarn:

Round 1: Sc 6 in a magic ring. [6 sts]

Round 2: Inc around. [12 sts]

Round 3: *Sc, inc; rep from * 5 more times. [18 sts]

Round 4: *Sc 2, inc; rep from * 5 more times. [24 sts]

Round 5: *Sc 3, inc; rep from * 5 more times. [30 sts]

Round 6: *Sc 4, inc; rep from * 5 more times. [36 sts]

Round 7: *Sc 5, inc; rep from * 5 more times. [42 sts]

Round 8: *Sc 6, inc; rep from * 5 more times. [48 sts]

Rounds 9–18: Sc around. [48 sts]

Round 19: *Sc 6, dec; rep from * 5 more times. [42 sts]

Round 20: *Sc 5, dec; rep from * 5 more times. [36 sts]

Round 21: *Sc 4, dec; rep from * 5 more times. [30 sts]

Begin stuffing the body and continue to add stuffing as you crochet the remaining rounds.

Round 22: *Sc 3, dec; rep from * 5 more times. [24 sts]

Round 23: *Sc 2, dec; rep from * 5 more times. [18 sts]

Round 24: *Sc, dec; rep from * 5 more times. [12 sts]

Round 25: Dec around. [6 sts]

Finish off and close up the hole.

EYES (MAKE 2):

Using Bright Yellow yarn:

Round 1: Sc 5 in a magic ring. [5 sts]

Round 2: Inc around. [10 sts]

Round 3: *Sc, inc; rep from * 4 more times. [15 sts]

Round 4: *Sc 2, inc; rep from * 4 more times. [20 sts]

Finish off, leaving a long end. Insert the safety eyes through the middle of each eye patch and secure with the safety eye washers. Sew the eye patches to the body under Round 6. They should be placed close together (almost touching in the middle).

BEAK:

Using Carrot yarn:

Round 1: Sc 4 in a magic ring. [4 sts]

Round 2: *Sc, inc; rep from * 1 more time. [6 sts]

Round 3: *Sc 2, inc; rep from * 1 more time. [8 sts]

Round 4: *Sc 3, inc; rep from * 1 more time. [10 sts]

Round 5: *Sc 4, inc; rep from * 1 more time. [12 sts]

Round 6: *Sc 5, inc; rep from * 1 more time. [14 sts]

Finish off, leaving a long end. Stuff the beak lightly and press the edges together to form a triangle shape. Sew the beak to the face just under and between the eyes.

EARS (MAKE 2):

Using Taupe yarn:

Round 1: Sc 4 in a magic ring. [4 sts]

Round 2: *Sc, inc; rep from * 1 more time. [6 sts]

Round 3: *Sc 2, inc; rcp from * 1 more time. [8 sts]

Round 4: *Sc 3, inc; rep from * 1 more time. [10 sts]

Round 5: *Sc 4, inc; rep from * 1 more time. [12 sts]

Round 6: Sc around. [12 sts]

Finish off, leaving a long end. Stuff the ears lightly and press the edges together to form a triangle shape. Sew the ears to the top of the body under Round 3.

WINGS (MAKE 2):

Using Taupe yarn:

Round 1: Sc 6 in a magic ring. [6 sts]

Round 2: Inc around. [12 sts]

Round 3: *Sc, inc; rep from * 5 more times. [18 sts]

Round 4: *Sc 2, inc; rep from * 5 more times. [24 sts]

Rounds 5–7: Sc around. [24 sts]

Round 8: *Sc 6, dec; rep from * 2 more times. [21 sts]

Round 9: Sc around. [21 sts]

Round 10: *Sc 5, dec; rep from * 2 more times. [18 sts]

Round 11: Sc around. [18 sts]

Round 12: *Sc 4, dec; rep from * 2 more times. [15 sts]

Round 13: Sc around. [15 sts]

Round 14: *Sc 3, dec; rep from * 2 more times. [12 sts]

Finish off, leaving a long end. Do not stuff. Instead, press the open edges together to flatten the wing, and then sew straight across the opening to close it up. Sew the wings to the sides of the body. The top of the wings should be level with Round 11, and they should be equally placed on either side of the body.

POPPY THE POPULAR PENGUIN

Poppy is the life of every party in the colony. When the long, dark nights of Antarctica get the other penguins down, she can always be counted on to cheer everyone up with a fun dance party. This quick and easy pattern uses many of the same components as Olympia the Offbeat Owl, so you can whip up a big penguin dance party in no time.

Size: 3½ inches high

MATERIALS:

Bernat Super Value medium 4 (100% acrylic; 426 yards (389 m)/197 g): Black, 70 yards

White, 25 yards

Carrot, 6 yards

US size G-6 (4.00 mm) crochet hook

2 (12-mm) black safety eyes

Polyester fiberfill

Tapestry needle

Removable stitch marker

STITCHES USED:

Magic ring

Single crochet (sc)

Increase (inc)

Decrease (dec)

BODY:

Using Black yarn:

Round 1: Sc 6 in a magic ring. [6 sts]

Round 2: Inc around. [12 sts]

Round 3: *Sc, inc; rep from * 5 more times. [18 sts]

Round 4: *Sc 2, inc; rep from * 5 more times. [24 sts]

Round 5: *Sc 3, inc; rep from * 5 more times. [30 sts]

Round 6: *Sc 4, inc; rep from * 5 more times. [36 sts]

Round 7: *Sc 5, inc; rep from * 5 more times. [42 sts]

Round 8: *Sc 6, inc; rep from * 5 more times. [48 sts]

Rounds 9–17: Sc around. [48 sts]

Switch to White yarn:

Round 18: Sc around. [48 sts]

Round 19: *Sc 6, dec; rep from * 5 more times. [42 sts]

Round 20: *Sc 5, dec; rep from * 5 more times. [36 sts]

Round 21: *Sc 4, dec; rep from * 5 more times. [30 sts]

Begin stuffing the body and continue to add stuffing as you crochet the remaining rounds.

Round 22: *Sc 3, dec; rep from * 5 more times. [24 sts]

Round 23: *Sc 2, dec; rep from * 5 more times. [18 sts]

Round 24: *Sc, dec; rep from * 5 more times. [12 sts]

Round 25: Dec around. [6 sts]

Finish off and close up the hole.

EYES (MAKE 2):

Using White yarn:

Round 1: Sc 5 in a magic ring. [5 sts]

Round 2: Inc around. [10 sts]

Round 3: *Sc, inc; rep from * 4 more times. [15 sts]

Round 4: *Sc 2, inc; rep from * 4 more times. [20 sts]

Finish off, leaving a long end. Insert the safety eyes through the middle of each eye patch and secure with the safety eye washers. Sew the eye patches to the body under Round 6. They should be placed close together (almost touching in the middle).

BEAK:

Using Carrot yarn:

Round 1: Sc 4 in a magic ring. [4 sts]

Round 2: *Sc, inc; rep from * 1 more time. [6 sts]

Round 3: *Sc 2, inc; rep from * 1 more time. [8 sts]

Round 4: *Sc 3, inc; rep from * 1 more time. [10 sts]

Round 5: *Sc 4, inc; rep from * 1 more time. [12 sts]

Round 6: *Sc 5, inc; rep from * 1 more time. [14 sts]

Finish off, leaving a long end. Stuff the beak lightly and press the edges together to form a triangle shape. Sew the beak to the face just under and between the eyes.

FLIPPERS (MAKE 2):

Using Black yarn:

Round 1: Sc 6 in a magic ring. [6 sts]

Round 2: Inc around. [12 sts]

Round 3: *Sc, inc; rep from * 5 more times. [18 sts]

Round 4: *Sc 2, inc; rep from * 5 more times. [24 sts]

Rounds 5–7: Sc around. [24 sts]

Round 8: *Sc 6, dec; rep from * 2 more times. [21 sts]

Round 9: Sc around. [21 sts]

Round 10: *Sc 5, dec; rep from * 2 more times. [18 sts]

Round 11: Sc around. [18 sts]

Round 12: *Sc 4, dec; rep from * 2 more times. [15 sts]

Round 13: Sc around. [15 sts]

Round 14: *Sc 3, dec; rep from * 2 more times. [12 sts]

Finish off, leaving a long end. Do not stuff. Instead, press the open edges together to flatten the flipper, and then sew straight across the opening to close it up. Sew the flippers to the sides of the body. The top of the flippers should be level with Round 11, and they should be equally placed on either side of the body.

CHARLIE THE CURIOUS ORCA

Charlie loves exploring the many bays and inlets along the rugged west coast of British Columbia. Sometimes, his curiosity gets the better of him and he swims into a sticky situation, but his family always finds him and brings him home. Charlie introduces a new technique to make his two-pronged tail. This may seem complicated at first, but go slowly and you'll get the hang of it soon.

Size: 4½ inches high

MATERIALS:

Bernat Super Value medium 4 (100% acrylic; 426 yards (389 m)/197 g): Black, 75 yards

White, 25 yards

US size G-6 (4.00 mm) crochet hook

2 (12-mm) black safety eyes

Polyester fiberfill

Tapestry needle

Removable stitch marker

STITCHES USED:

Magic ring

Single crochet (sc)

Double crochet (dc)

Increase (inc)

Decrease (dec)

Double crochet increase (dc inc)—This is just like a normal increase, but instead of working two single crochets into one stitch, you will work two double crochets into one stitch.

BODY:

Using Black yarn:

Round 1: Sc 6 in a magic ring. [6 sts]
Round 2: Inc around. [12 sts]
Round 3: *Sc, inc; rep from * 5 more times. [18 sts]
Round 4: *Sc 2, inc; rep from * 5 more times. [24 sts]
Round 5: *Sc 3, inc; rep from * 5 more times. [30 sts]
Round 6: *Sc 4, inc; rep from * 5 more times. [36 sts]
Round 7: *Sc 5, inc; rep from * 5 more times. [42 sts]
Round 8: *Sc 6, inc; rep from * 5 more times. [48 sts]
Rounds 9–17: Sc around. [48 sts]

Switch to White yarn:

Round 18: Sc around. [48 sts]
Round 19: *Sc 6, dec; rep from * 5 more times. [42 sts]
Round 20: *Sc 5, dec; rep from * 5 more times. [36 sts]
Round 21: *Sc 4, dec; rep from * 5 more times. [30 sts]

Begin stuffing the body and continue to add stuffing as you crochet the remaining rounds.

Round 22: *Sc 3, dec; rep from * 5 more times. [24 sts]
Round 23: *Sc 2, dec; rep from * 5 more times. [18 sts]
Round 24: *Sc, dec; rep from * 5 more times. [12 sts]
Round 25: Dec around. [6 sts]

Finish off and close up the hole.

EYES (MAKE 2):

Using White yarn:

Round 1: Sc 6 in a magic ring. [6 sts]

Round 2: Inc 3, dc inc 2, inc. [12 sts]

Round 3: *Sc, inc; rep from * 2 more times; *dc, dc inc; rep from * 1 more time; sc, inc. [18 sts]

Finish off, leaving a long end. You will notice that the hole from Round 1 is not directly in the middle of the eye patch, because we added the taller double crochet stitch on one side of the eye. This is correct, and gives the eye patch its oval shape with the safety eye offset to one side.

Insert the safety eyes through the Round 1 hole of each eye patch and secure with the safety eye washers. Sew the eye patches to the body under Round 9 and about six stitches apart. The side with the safety eye should be toward the front of the head, and the bottom of the eye patch should be about three rounds above the white belly.

TOP FIN:

Using Black yarn:

Round 1: Sc 4 in a magic ring. [4 sts]

Round 2: *Sc, inc; rep from * 1 more time. [6 sts]

Round 3: *Sc 2, inc; rep from * 1 more time. [8 sts]

Round 4: *Sc 3, inc; rep from * 1 more time. [10 sts]

Round 5: *Sc 4, inc; rep from * 1 more time. [12 sts]

Round 6: Sc around. [12 sts]

Round 7: *Sc 5, inc; rep from * 1 more time. [14 sts]

Round 8: Sc around. [14 sts]

Finish off, leaving a long end. Stuff the top fin lightly and press the edges together to form a triangle shape. Sew the fin to the top of the body, right over the middle hole from Round 1 of the body. The fin should face forward and be evenly placed between the eyes.

SIDE FLIPPERS (MAKE 2):

Using Black yarn:

Round 1: Sc 6 in a magic ring. [6 sts]

Round 2: Inc around. [12 sts]

Round 3: *Sc, inc; rep from * 5 more times. [18 sts]

Rounds 4–5: Sc around. [18 sts]

Round 6: *Sc 4, dec; rep from * 2 more times. [15 sts]

Round 7: Sc around. [15 sts]

Round 8: *Sc 3, dec; rep from * 2 more times. [12 sts]

Round 9: Sc around. [12 sts]

Round 10: *Sc 2, dec; rep from * 2 more times. [9 sts]

Finish off, leaving a long end. Do not stuff. Instead, press the open edges together to flatten the flipper, and then sew straight across the opening to close it up. Sew the flippers to the sides of the body, just behind the eyes. The flippers should be roughly level with the bottom of the eye pieces.

TAIL:

The tail is made up of two fin pieces that are then crocheted together to make the base of the tail.

Using Black yarn:

Round 1: Sc 6 in a magic ring. [6 sts]

Round 2: *Sc, inc; rep from * 2 more times. [9 sts]

Round 3: *Sc 2, inc; rep from * 2 more times. [12 sts]

Round 4: *Sc 3, inc; rep from * 2 more times. [15 sts]

Rounds 5–6: Sc around. [15 sts]

Cut your yarn, leaving a long end, and pull the end through the loop on your hook. Set this first fin aside.

Repeat Rounds 1 to 6 to make a second fin. Do not finish off or cut the yarn.

Round 7: You are now going to join the two fins together, and then continue to crochet the remaining rounds of the tail. Follow these steps:

Step 1: Hold the open edges of the first and second fins next to each other. Your hook will still be in the final loop from Round 6 of the second fin.

Step 2: Insert your hook into the next unworked stitch of the first fin and complete one sc. Place your stitch marker in the Sc you just made; this will be the first stitch of your new round. Sc 14 more stitches around the first fin.

Step 3: Insert your hook into the next unworked stitch of the second fin and complete one sc. Sc 14 more stitches around the second fin.

The two fins will now be joined together, and you will have completed 30 stitches around. There will be a bit of a gap between the two fins, but you can sew that up later once the tail is finished and stuffed.

Round 8: Sc around. [30 sts]

Round 9: *Sc 3, dec; rep from * 5 more times. [24 sts]

Stuff the fins lightly. Continue to stuff as you crochet the remaining rounds of the tail. Do not stuff too firmly, as the tail should remain slightly flat and not bulge out too much.

Round 10: *Sc 2, dec; rep from * 5 more times. [18 sts]

Round 11: *Sc 4, dec; rep from * 2 more times. [15 sts]

Round 12: Sc around. [15 sts]

Finish off, leaving a long end. Sew the tail to the back of the orca, along the line of the color change from black to white.

SIDE PATCHES (MAKE 2):

Using White yarn:

Round 1: Sc 6 in a magic ring. [6 sts]

Round 2: Inc around. [12 sts]

Finish off, leaving a long end. Sew the side patches to the orca between the side flippers and the tail.

DIETER THE DARING DACHSHUND

Dieter loves running through the forests surrounding Berlin with his human, chasing rabbits and burrowing into badger holes. Sometimes, however, his daring nature gets him into trouble and he bites off more than he can chew—like the time he tried to take on a wild boar, and barely escaped with his life! Dieter is the perfect gift for dog lovers. He's easy to make, and oh so cute.

Size: 11½ inches long, 7 inches high

MATERIALS:

Bernat Super Value medium 4 (100% acrylic; 426 yards (389 m)/197 g): Walnut, 220 yards

US size G-6 (4.00 mm) crochet hook

2 (12-mm) black safety eyes

1 (15-mm) black safety nose

Polyester fiberfill

Tapestry needle

Removable stitch marker

STITCHES USED:

Magic ring

Single crochet (sc)

Increase (inc)

Decrease (inc)

HEAD:

Using Walnut yarn:

Round 1: Sc 6 in a magic ring. [6 sts]

Round 2: Inc around. [12 sts]

Round 3: *Sc, inc; rep from * 5 more times. [18 sts]

Round 4: *Sc 2, inc; rep from * 5 more times. [24 sts]

Round 5: *Sc 3, inc; rep from * 5 more times. [30 sts]

Round 6: *Sc 4, inc; rep from * 5 more times. [36 sts]

Round 7: *Sc 5, inc; rep from * 5 more times. [42 sts]

Rounds 8–16: Sc around. [42 sts]

Round 17: *Sc 5, dec; rep from * 5 more times. [36 sts]

Round 18: *Sc 4, dec; rep from * 5 more times. [30 sts]

Insert the safety eyes between Rounds 10 and 11, about six stitches apart. Begin stuffing the head and continue to add stuffing as you crochet the remaining rounds.

Round 19: *Sc 3, dec; rep from * 5 more times. [24 sts]

Round 20: *Sc 2, dec; rep from * 5 more times. [18 sts]

Round 21: *Sc, dec; rep from * 5 more times. [12 sts]

Finish off, leaving a long end, which you will use to sew the head to the body.

SNOUT:

Using Walnut yarn:

Round 1: Sc 6 in a magic ring. [6 sts]

Round 2: Inc around. [12 sts]

Rounds 3–4: Sc around. [12 sts]

Round 5: *Sc 3, inc; rep from * 2 more times. [15 sts]

Rounds 6–7: Sc around. [15 sts]

Insert the safety nose between Rounds 1 and 2. The flat part of the nose should be facing up, and the bottom of the nose should be pointing down to the middle hole from Round 1.

Round 8: *Sc 4, inc; rep from * 2 more times. [18 sts]

Rounds 9–10: Sc around. [18 sts]

Round 11: *Sc 5, inc; rep from * 2 more times. [21 sts]

Rounds 12–13: Sc around. [21 sts]

Round 14: *Sc 6, inc; rep from * 2 more times. [24 sts]

Finish off, leaving a long end. Stuff the snout, and then sew it to the front of the head just beneath the eyes. Make sure the snout is positioned so that the nose is facing up.

EARS (MAKE 2):

Using Walnut yarn:

Round 1: Sc 6 in a magic ring. [6 sts]

Round 2: Inc around. [12 sts]

Round 3: *Sc, inc; rep from * 5 more times. [18 sts]

Round 4: *Sc 2, inc; rep from * 5 more times. [24 sts]

Rounds 5–7: Sc around. [24 sts]

Round 8: *Sc 6, dec; rep from * 2 more times. [21 sts]

Rounds 9–10: Sc around. [21 sts]

Round 11: *Sc 5, dec; rep from * 2 more times. [18 sts]

Rounds 12–13: Sc around. [18 sts]

Round 14: *Sc 4, dec; rep from * 2 more times. [15 sts]

Rounds 15–16: Sc around. [15 sts]

Finish off, leaving a long end. Do not stuff. Instead, press the open edges together to flatten the ear, and then sew straight across the opening to close it up. Sew the ears on so they are equally placed on either side of the head below Round 9.

BODY:

Using Walnut yarn:

Round 1: Sc 6 in a magic ring. [6 sts]

Round 2: Inc around. [12 sts]

Round 3: *Sc, inc; rep from * 5 more times. [18 sts]

Round 4: *Sc 2, inc; rep from * 5 more times. [24 sts]

Round 5: *Sc 3, inc; rep from * 5 more times. [30 sts]

Round 6: *Sc 4, inc; rep from * 5 more times. [36 sts]

Stuff the body as you work the following rounds. Do not leave the stuffing until the end, because it will be difficult to stuff Dieter's long body if you wait.

Rounds 7–41: Sc around. [36 sts]

Round 42: *Sc 4, dec; rep from * 5 more times. [30 sts]

Round 43: *Sc 3, dec; rep from * 5 more times. [24 sts]

Round 44: *Sc 2, dec; rep from * 5 more times. [18 sts]

Round 45: *Sc, dec; rep from * 5 more times. [12 sts]

Round 46: Dec around. [6 sts]

Finish off and close up the hole. Sew the head on at the front of the body.

LEGS (MAKE 4):

Using Walnut yarn:

Round 1: Sc 6 in a magic ring. [6 sts]

Round 2: Inc around. [12 sts]

Round 3: *Sc, inc; rep from * 5 more times. [18 sts]

Rounds 4–6: Sc around. [18 sts]

Round 7: Dec 6, sc 6. [12 sts]

Rounds 8–10: Sc around. [12 sts]

Finish off, leaving a long end. Stuff the legs firmly. Sew two legs at the front of the body and two legs at the back of the body, making sure that the feet curve forward.

TAIL:

Using Walnut yarn:

Round 1: Sc 6 in a magic ring. [6 sts]

Round 2: *Sc, inc; rep from * 2 more times. [9 sts]

Rounds 3–11: Sc around. [9 sts]

Finish off, leaving a long end. Stuff the tail lightly and sew it to the back of the body, pointing upward.

CALLIE THE CREATIVE CATERPILLAR

Callie's greatest dream is to become an artist and have her work exhibited at the Metropolitan Museum of Art. She loves the beautiful colors and shapes of abstract art, which remind her of the butterfly she will one day become. Unfortunately, holding a paintbrush is tricky for a tiny caterpillar, but she perseveres and never loses sight of her goal. Callie's body is made in one piece by using simple shaping to create four conjoined spheres. By the time you finish, you will be an expert at increasing and decreasing.

Size: 12 inches long, 7½ inches high

MATERIALS:
Bernat Super Value medium 4 (100% acrylic; 426 yards (389 m)/197 g): Lush, 150 yards
Black, 45 yards
US size G-6 (4.00 mm) crochet hook
2 (12-mm) black safety eyes
Polyester fiberfill
Tapestry needle
Removable stitch marker

STITCHES USED:
Magic ring
Single crochet (sc)
Increase (inc)
Decrease (dec)

HEAD:

Using Lush yarn:

Round 1: Sc 6 in a magic ring. [6 sts]

Round 2: Inc around. [12 sts]

Round 3: *Sc, inc; rep from * 5 more times. [18 sts]

Round 4: *Sc 2, inc; rep from * 5 more times. [24 sts]

Round 5: *Sc 3, inc; rep from * 5 more times. [30 sts]

Round 6: *Sc 4, inc; rep from * 5 more times. [36 sts]

Round 7: *Sc 5, inc; rep from * 5 more times. [42 sts]

Rounds 8–16: Sc around. [42 sts]

Round 17: *Sc 5, dec; rep from * 5 more times. [36 sts]

Round 18: *Sc 4, dec; rep from * 5 more times. [30 sts]

Insert the safety eyes between Rounds 11 and 12, about six stitches apart. Begin stuffing the head and continue to add stuffing as you crochet the remaining rounds.

Round 19: *Sc 3, dec; rep from * 5 more times. [24 sts]

Round 20: *Sc 2, dec; rep from * 5 more times. [18 sts]

Round 21: *Sc, dec; rep from * 5 more times. [12 sts]

Finish off, leaving a long end, which you will use to sew the head to the body.

ANTENNAE (MAKE 2):

Using Black yarn:

Round 1: Sc 6 in a magic ring. [6 sts]

Round 2: Inc around. [12 sts]

Rounds 3–5: Sc around. [12 sts]

Round 6: *Sc, dec; rep from * 3 more times. [8 sts]

Stuff the tips of the antennae and continue to add stuffing as you crochet the remaining rounds.

Rounds 7–11: Sc around. [8 sts]

Finish off, leaving a long end. Sew the antennae to the head, just below Round 3. They should be evenly placed on either side of the head and in line with the eyes.

BODY:

Using Lush yarn:

Round 1: Sc 6 in a magic ring. [6 sts]

Round 2: Inc around. [12 sts]

Round 3: *Sc, inc; rep from * 5 more times. [18 sts]

Round 4: *Sc 2, inc; rep from * 5 more times. [24 sts]

Round 5: *Sc 3, inc; rep from * 5 more times. [30 sts]

Round 6: *Sc 4, inc; rep from * 5 more times. [36 sts]

Rounds 7–14: Sc around. [36 sts]

Round 15: *Sc 4, dec; rep from * 5 more times. [30 sts]

Begin stuffing the first ball of the body and continue to add stuffing as you crochet each remaining ball.

Round 16: *Sc 3, dec; rep from * 5 more times. [24 sts]

Round 17: *Sc 2, dec; rep from * 5 more times. [18 sts]

Round 18: *Sc 2, inc; rep from * 5 more times. [24 sts]

Round 19: *Sc 3, inc; rep from * 5 more times. [30 sts]

Round 20: *Sc 4, inc; rep from * 5 more times. [36 sts]

Rounds 21–28: Sc around. [36 sts]

Round 29: *Sc 4, dec; rep from * 5 more times. [30 sts]

Round 30: *Sc 3, dec; rep from * 5 more times. [24 sts]

Round 31: *Sc 2, dec; rep from * 5 more times. [18 sts]

Round 32: *Sc 2, inc; rep from * 5 more times. [24 sts]

Round 33: *Sc 3, inc; rep from * 5 more times. [30 sts]

Round 34: *Sc 4, inc; rep from * 5 more times. [36 sts]

Rounds 35–42: Sc around. [36 sts]

Round 43: *Sc 4, dec; rep from * 5 more times. [30 sts]

Round 44: *Sc 3, dec; rep from * 5 more times. [24 sts]

Round 45: *Sc 2, dec; rep from * 5 more times. [18 sts]

Round 46: *Sc 2, inc; rep from * 5 more times. [24 sts]

Round 47: *Sc 3, inc; rep from * 5 more times. [30 sts]

Round 48: *Sc 4, inc; rep from * 5 more times. [36 sts]

Rounds 49–56: Sc around. [36 sts]

Round 57: *Sc 4, dec; rep from * 5 more times. [30 sts]

Round 58: *Sc 3, dec; rep from * 5 more times. [24 sts]

Round 59: *Sc 2, dec; rep from * 5 more times. [18 sts]

Round 60: *Sc, dec; rep from * 5 more times. [12 sts]

Round 61: Dec around. [6 sts]

Finish off and close up the hole. Sew the head on top of the body, at the front of the first ball.

LEGS (MAKE 8):

Using Black yarn:

Round 1: Sc 6 in a magic ring. [6 sts]

Round 2: Inc around. [12 sts]

Rounds 3–5: Sc around. [12 sts]

Round 6: *Sc 2, dec; rep from * 2 more times. [9 sts]

Finish off, leaving a long end, and stuff the legs. Sew two legs to each ball of the body. The legs should be positioned midway along each ball, and about five stitches apart.

SAMMY THE SPEEDY SEA TURTLE

Most turtles aren't known for their speed, but Sammy loves to go fast. He always swims at the front of the group and urges his fellow turtles on. Whenever his flippers get tired, Sammy catches a ride in the swift currents of the Pacific Ocean. To make the ridge of Sammy's shell, you will crochet one round into the back loop only (BLO) and then work a round into the leftover front loops. Refer here for instructions on how to crochet in the back and front loops.

Size: 8½ inches long

MATERIALS:

Bernat Super Value medium 4 (100% acrylic; 426 yards (389 m)/197 g): Chocolate, 35 yards

Topaz, 20 yards

Lush, 100 yards

US size G-6 (4.00 mm) crochet hook

2 (12-mm) black safety eyes

Polyester fiberfill

Tapestry needle

Removable stitch marker

STITCHES USED:

Magic ring

Slip stitch (sl st)

Single crochet (sc)

Increase (inc)

Decrease (dec)

Back loop only (BLO)

BODY AND SHELL:

Using Chocolate yarn:

Round 1: Sc 6 in a magic ring. [6 sts]

Round 2: Inc around. [12 sts]

Round 3: *Sc, inc; rep from * 5 more times. [18 sts]

Round 4: *Sc 2, inc; rep from * 5 more times. [24 sts]

Round 5: *Sc 3, inc; rep from * 5 more times. [30 sts]

Round 6: *Sc 4, inc; rep from * 5 more times. [36 sts]

Round 7: *Sc 5, inc; rep from * 5 more times. [42 sts]

Round 8: *Sc 6, inc; rep from * 5 more times. [48 sts]

Round 9: *Sc 7, inc; rep from * 5 more times. [54 sts]

Rounds 10–12: Sc around. [54 sts]

Switch to Topaz yarn:

Round 13: Working in the back loop only (BLO), sc around. [54 sts]

Round 14: *Sc 7, dec; rep from * 5 more times. [48 sts]

Round 15: *Sc 6, dec; rep from * 5 more times. [42 sts]

Round 16: *Sc 5, dec; rep from * 5 more times. [36 sts]

Round 17: *Sc 4, dec; rep from * 5 more times. [30 sts]

Round 18: *Sc 3, dec; rep from * 5 more times. [24 sts]

Begin stuffing the body and continue to add stuffing as you crochet the remaining rounds.

Round 19: *Sc 2, dec; rep from * 5 more times. [18 sts]

Round 20: *Sc, dec; rep from * 5 more times. [12 sts]

Round 21: Dec around. [6 sts]

Finish off and close up the hole.

Next, you will crochet one round into the leftover front loop from Round 13 to make a ridge. Follow these steps:

Step 1: Using Chocolate yarn, make a slip knot on your hook.

Step 2: Insert your hook from top to bottom into the first front loop from Round 13. You will be working around the shell in a counterclockwise direction.

Step 3: Sc around [54 sts], then sl st into the first stitch of the round and finish off.

HEAD:

Using Lush yarn:

Round 1: Sc 6 in a magic ring. [6 sts]

Round 2: Inc around. [12 sts]

Round 3: *Sc, inc; rep from * 5 more times. [18 sts]

Round 4: *Sc 2, inc; rep from * 5 more times. [24 sts]

Round 5: *Sc 3, inc; rep from * 5 more times. [30 sts]

Round 6: *Sc 4, inc; rep from * 5 more times. [36 sts]

Rounds 7–13: Sc around. [36 sts]

Round 14: *Sc 4, dec; rep from * 5 more times. [30 sts]

Insert the safety eyes between Rounds 5 and 6, about ten stitches apart. Begin stuffing the head and continue to add stuffing as you crochet the remaining rounds. The head should be stuffed firmly, and the neck should be stuffed lightly.

Round 15: *Sc 3, dec; rep from * 5 more times. [24 sts]

Round 16: *Sc 2, dec; rep from * 5 more times. [18 sts]

Rounds 17–23: Sc around. [18 sts]

Finish off, leaving a long end. Press the open edges together to flatten the top of the neck, and then sew straight across the opening to close it up. Sew the neck to the underside of the shell, about four rounds below the dark brown top shell. Add a few stitches between the back of the neck and the shell to ensure the neck is stable and doesn't flop down.

FLIPPERS (MAKE 4):

Using Lush yarn:

Round 1: Sc 6 in a magic ring. [6 sts]

Round 2: *Sc, inc; rep from * 2 more times. [9 sts]

Round 3: Sc around. [9 sts]

Round 4: *Sc 2, inc; rep from * 2 more times. [12 sts]

Round 5: Sc around. [12 sts]

Round 6: *Sc 3, inc; rep from * 2 more times. [15 sts]

Round 7: Sc around. [15 sts]

Round 8: *Sc 4, inc; rep from * 2 more times. [18 sts]

Rounds 9–13: Sc around. [18 sts]

Stuff the flipper lightly and continue stuffing as you crochet the remaining rounds.

Round 14: *Sc 4, dec; rep from * 2 more times. [15 sts]

Round 15: Sc around. [15 sts]

Round 16: *Sc 3, dec; rep from * 2 more times. [12 sts]

Round 17: Sc around. [12 sts]

Finish off, leaving a long end. Press the open edges together to flatten the top of the flipper. Sew straight across the opening to close it up, and then sew the flippers to the underside of the shell. Make sure to leave a space between the back flippers for the tail.

TAIL:

Using Lush yarn:

Round 1: Sc 6 in a magic ring. [6 sts]

Round 2: *Sc, inc; rep from * 2 more times. [9 sts]

Rounds 3–5: Sc around. [9 sts]

Round 6: *Sc 2, inc; rep from * 2 more times. [12 sts]

Rounds 7–9: Sc around. [12 sts]

Finish off, leaving a long end. Stuff lightly, then press the open edges together to flatten the top of the tail. Sew straight across the opening to close it up, and then sew the tail to the underside of the shell between the back flippers.

FLORA THE FANCIFUL FLAMINGO

Whenever Flora gets bored of her life in Tanzania's Lake Natron, she closes her eyes and lets a flight of fancy whisk her off to faraway lands. Whispered rumors tell of other flamingos living on white sand beaches under swaying palm trees, and she dreams of one day visiting to see for herself.

Size: 7½ inches high

MATERIALS:

Bernat Super Value medium 4 (100% acrylic; 426 yards (389 m)/197 g): Peony Pink, 105 yards

Black, 1 yard

Baby Pink (light pink), 36 yards

US size G-6 (4.00 mm) crochet hook

2 (12-mm) black safety eyes

Polyester fiberfill

Tapestry needle

Removable stitch marker

STITCHES USED:

Magic ring

Single crochet (sc)

Increase (inc)

Decrease (dec)

HEAD, NECK, AND BODY:

The head, neck, and body are worked in one continuous piece, starting at the top of the head.

Using Peony Pink yarn:

Round 1: Sc 6 in a magic ring. [6 sts]

Round 2: Inc around. [12 sts]

Round 3: *Sc, inc; rep from * 5 more times. [18 sts]

Round 4: *Sc 2, inc; rep from * 5 more times. [24 sts]

Round 5: *Sc 3, inc; rep from * 5 more times. [30 sts]

Round 6: *Sc 4, inc; rep from * 5 more times. [36 sts]

Rounds 7–13: Sc around. [36 sts]

Round 14: *Sc 4, dec; rep from * 5 more times. [30 sts]

Insert the safety eyes between Rounds 9 and 10, about five stitches apart. Begin stuffing the head and continue to add stuffing as you crochet the remaining rounds.

Round 15: *Sc 3, dec; rep from * 5 more times. [24 sts]

Round 16: *Sc 2, dec; rep from * 5 more times. [18 sts]

Rounds 17–24: Sc around. [18 sts]

Round 25: *Sc 2, inc; rep from * 5 more times. [24 sts]

Round 26: Sc around. [24 sts]

Round 27: *Sc 3, inc; rep from * 5 more times. [30 sts]

Round 28: Sc around. [30 sts]

Round 29: *Sc 4, inc; rep from * 5 more times. [36 sts]

Round 30: *Sc 5, inc; rep from * 5 more times. [42 sts]

Rounds 31–38: Sc around. [42 sts]

Round 39: *Sc 5, dec; rep from * 5 more times. [36 sts]

Round 40: *Sc 4, dec; rep from * 5 more times. [30 sts]

Round 41: *Sc 3, dec; rep from * 5 more times. [24 sts]

Round 42: *Sc 2, dec; rep from * 5 more times. [18 sts]

Round 43: *Sc, dec; rep from * 5 more times. [12 sts]

Round 44: Dec around. [6 sts]

Finish off and sew up the hole.

BEAK:

Using Black yarn:

Round 1: Sc 6 in a magic ring. [6 sts]

Round 2: Sc around. [6 sts]

Round 3: *Sc, inc; rep from * 2 more times. [9 sts]

Rounds 4–5: Sc around. [9 sts]

Switch to Baby Pink yarn:

Round 6: Sc around. [9 sts]

Round 7: *Sc 2, inc; rep from * 2 more times. [12 sts]

Round 8: Sc around. [12 sts]

Finish off, leaving a long end. Sew the beak to the face, just below the eyes.

WINGS (MAKE 2):

Using Peony Pink yarn:

Round 1: Sc 6 in a magic ring. [6 sts]

Round 2: Sc around. [6 sts]

Round 3: *Sc, inc; rep from * 2 more times. [9 sts]

Round 4: Sc around. [9 sts]

Round 5: *Sc 2, inc; rep from * 2 more times. [12 sts]

Round 6: Sc around. [12 sts]

Round 7: *Sc 3, inc; rep from * 2 more times. [15 sts]

Round 8: Sc around. [15 sts]

Round 9: *Sc 4, inc; rep from * 2 more times. [18 sts]

Round 10: Sc around. [18 sts]

Round 11: *Sc 5, inc; rep from * 2 more times. [21 sts]

Rounds 12–15: Sc around. [21 sts]

Round 16: *Sc 5, dec; rep from * 2 more times. [18 sts]

Round 17: *Sc, dec; rep from * 5 more times. [12 sts]

Round 18: Dec around. [6 sts]

Finish off, leaving a long end, and sew up the hole. Do not stuff. Instead, press the wing flat and then sew the wings to the sides of the body, with the wide part at the front and leaving the narrower end free to flap. The top of the wings should be level with Round 27, and they should be equally placed on either side of the body.

LEGS (MAKE 2):

Stuff the legs as you go.

Using Baby Pink yarn:

Round 1: Sc 6 in a magic ring. [6 sts]

Round 2: Inc around. [12 sts]

Round 3: *Sc, inc; rep from * 5 more times. [18 sts]

Rounds 4–5: Sc around. [18 sts]

Round 6: Dec 6, sc 6. [12 sts]

Round 7: Dec 3, sc 6. [9 sts]

Rounds 8–27: Sc around. [9 sts]

Finish off, leaving a long end. Press the open edges together to flatten the top of the leg, making sure that the foot curves upward. Sew straight across the opening to close it up, and then sew the legs to the front of the body.

FRANÇOIS THE FRIENDLY FROG

François loves to make friends with all his fellow animals in the Louisiana bayou he calls home—except for the alligators! He tried to befriend an alligator once, and almost got eaten. François hopes that one day his friendly nature will win the alligators over, but in the meantime he is keeping his distance. François and the next three patterns share the same basic body shapes, with different details such as ears, eyes, and tails.

Size: 7 inches high

MATERIALS:

Bernat Super Value medium 4 (100% acrylic; 426 yards (389 m)/197 g): Lush, 95 yards

Yellow, 20 yards

White, 12 yards

US size G-6 (4.00 mm) crochet hook

2 (12-mm) black safety eyes

Polyester fiberfill

Tapestry needle

Removable stitch marker

STITCHES USED:

Magic ring

Single crochet (sc)

Increase (inc)

Decrease (dec)

HEAD AND BODY:

The head and body are worked in one continuous piece, starting at the top of the head.

Using Lush yarn:

Round 1: Sc 6 in a magic ring. [6 sts]

Round 2: Inc around. [12 sts]

Round 3: *Sc, inc; rep from * 5 more times. [18 sts]

Round 4: *Sc 2, inc; rep from * 5 more times. [24 sts]

Round 5: *Sc 3, inc; rep from * 5 more times. [30 sts]

Round 6: *Sc 4, inc; rep from * 5 more times. [36 sts]

Round 7: *Sc 5, inc; rep from * 5 more times. [42 sts]

Rounds 8–14: Sc around. [42 sts]

Switch to Yellow yarn:

Rounds 15–16: Sc around. [42 sts]

Round 17: *Sc 5, dec; rep from * 5 more times. [36 sts]

Round 18: *Sc 4, dec; rep from * 5 more times. [30 sts]

Begin stuffing the head and continue to add stuffing as you crochet the remaining rounds.

Round 19: *Sc 3, dec; rep from * 5 more times. [24 sts]

Round 20: *Sc 2, dec; rep from * 5 more times. [18 sts]

Round 21: *Sc, dec; rep from * 5 more times. [12 sts]

Switch to Lush yarn:

Round 22: *Sc, inc; rep from * 5 more times. [18 sts]

Round 23: *Sc 2, inc; rep from * 5 more times. [24 sts]

Round 24: Sc around. [24 sts]

Round 25: *Sc 3, inc; rep from * 5 more times. [30 sts]

Round 26: Sc around. [30 sts]

Round 27: *Sc 4, inc; rep from * 5 more times. [36 sts]

Rounds 28–34: Sc around. [36 sts]

Round 35: *Sc 4, dec; rep from * 5 more times. [30 sts]

Round 36: *Sc 3, dec; rep from * 5 more times. [24 sts]

Round 37: *Sc 2, dec; rep from * 5 more times. [18 sts]

Round 38: *Sc, dec; rep from * 5 more times. [12 sts]

Round 39: Dec around. [6 sts]

Finish off and sew up the hole.

EYES (MAKE 2):

Using White yarn:

Round 1: Sc 7 in a magic ring. [7 sts]

Round 2: Inc around. [14 sts]

Rounds 3–6: Sc around. [14 sts]

Insert the safety eyes between Rounds 4 and 5. Stuff the eyeballs.

Round 7: Dec around. [7 sts]

Finish off, leaving a long end. Sew the eyes to the top front of the head, below Round 5.

ARMS (MAKE 2):

Using Lush yarn:

Round 1: Sc 6 in a magic ring. [6 sts]

Round 2: Inc around. [12 sts]

Round 3: *Sc 3, inc; rep from * 2 more times. [15 sts]

Rounds 4–6: Sc around. [15 sts]

Round 7: Dec 6, sc 3. [9 sts]

Rounds 8–13: Sc around. [9 sts]

Finish off, leaving a long end. Stuff the hand and lower arm firmly, and stuff the upper arm more lightly. Press the open edges together to flatten the top of the arm, making sure that the hand curves inward. Sew straight across the opening to close it up, and then sew the arms to the sides of the body a couple of rounds below the neck.

LEGS (MAKE 2):

Using Lush yarn:

Round 1: Sc 6 in a magic ring. [6 sts]

Round 2: Inc around. [12 sts]

Round 3: *Sc, inc; rep from * 5 more times. [18 sts]

Rounds 4–6: Sc around. [18 sts]

Round 7: Dec 6, sc 6. [12 sts]

Rounds 8–11: Sc around. [12 sts]

Finish off, leaving a long end. Stuff the foot and lower leg firmly, and stuff the upper leg more lightly. Sew the legs to the front of the body, making sure that the feet curve upward.

BELLY:

Using Yellow yarn:

Round 1: Sc 6 in a magic ring. [6 sts]

Round 2: Inc around. [12 sts]

Round 3: *Sc, inc; rep from * 5 more times. [18 sts]

Round 4: *Sc 2, inc; rep from * 5 more times. [24 sts]

Round 5: *Sc 3, inc; rep from * 5 more times. [30 sts]

Finish off, leaving a very long tail. Sew the belly onto the body.

YUKI THE ROMANTIC RABBIT

Yuki's favorite season is winter, and she loves hopping through her snow-covered garden in Kyoto. Winter is just so romantic. She can't wait until she meets the rabbit of her dreams, and they can hop side by side through the snow together!

Size: 6½ inches high

MATERIALS:

Bernat Super Value medium 4 (100% acrylic; 426 yards (389 m)/197 g): White, 150 yards

US size G-6 (4.00 mm) crochet hook

2 (12-mm) black safety eyes

1 (15-mm) pink safety nose

Polyester fiberfill

Tapestry needle

Removable stitch marker

STITCHES USED:

Magic ring

Single crochet (sc)

Increase (inc)

Decrease (inc)

HEAD AND BODY:

The head and body are worked in one continuous piece, starting at the top of the head.

Using White yarn:

Round 1: Sc 6 in a magic ring. [6 sts]

Round 2: Inc around. [12 sts]

Round 3: *Sc, inc; rep from * 5 more times. [18 sts]

Round 4: *Sc 2, inc; rep from * 5 more times. [24 sts]

Round 5: *Sc 3, inc; rep from * 5 more times. [30 sts]

Round 6: *Sc 4, inc; rep from * 5 more times. [36 sts]

Round 7: *Sc 5, inc; rep from * 5 more times. [42 sts]

Rounds 8–16: Sc around. [42 sts]

Round 17: *Sc 5, dec; rep from * 5 more times. [36 sts]

Round 18: *Sc 4, dec; rep from * 5 more times. [30 sts]

Insert the safety eyes between Rounds 11 and 12, about six stitches apart. Insert the safety nose between Rounds 14 and 15 and centered between the eyes. Begin stuffing the head and continue to add stuffing as you crochet the remaining rounds.

Round 19: *Sc 3, dec; rep from * 5 more times. [24 sts]

Round 20: *Sc 2, dec; rep from * 5 more times. [18 sts]

Round 21: *Sc, dec; rep from * 5 more times. [12 sts]

Round 22: *Sc, inc; rep from * 5 more times. [18 sts]

Round 23: *Sc 2, inc; rep from * 5 more times. [24 sts]

Round 24: Sc around. [24 sts]

Round 25: *Sc 3, inc; rep from * 5 more times. [30 sts]

Round 26: Sc around. [30 sts]

Round 27: *Sc 4, inc; rep from * 5 more times. [36 sts]

Rounds 28–34: Sc around. [36 sts]

Round 35: *Sc 4, dec; rep from * 5 more times. [30 sts]

Round 36: *Sc 3, dec; rep from * 5 more times. [24 sts]

Round 37: *Sc 2, dec; rep from * 5 more times. [18 sts]

Round 38: *Sc, dec; rep from * 5 more times. [12 sts]

Round 39: Dec around. [6 sts]

Finish off and sew up the hole.

EARS (MAKE 2):

Using White yarn:

Round 1: Sc 6 in a magic ring. [6 sts]

Round 2: *Sc, inc; rep from * 2 more times. [9 sts]

Round 3: *Sc 2, inc; rep from * 2 more times. [12 sts]

Round 4: *Sc 3, inc; rep from * 2 more times. [15 sts]

Round 5: *Sc 4, inc; rep from * 2 more times. [18 sts]

Round 6: *Sc 5, inc; rep from * 2 more times. [21 sts]

Rounds 7–8: Sc around. [21 sts]

Round 9: *Sc 5, dec; rep from * 2 more times. [18 sts]

Rounds 10–11: Sc around. [18 sts]

Round 12: *Sc 7, dec; rep from * 1 more time. [16 sts]

Rounds 13–14: Sc around. [16 sts]

Round 15: *Sc 6, dec; rep from * 1 more time. [14 sts]

Rounds 16–17: Sc around. [14 sts]

Round 18: *Sc 5, dec; rep from * 1 more time. [12 sts]

Rounds 19–20: Sc around. [12 sts]

Round 21: *Sc 4, dec; rep from * 1 more time. [10 sts]

Rounds 22–23: Sc around. [10 sts]

Finish off, leaving a long end. Do not stuff. Press the open edges together to flatten the ear, then sew straight across the opening to close it up. Sew the ears on so they are equally placed on either side of the head below Round 3. Finally, make a few stitches between the back of the ear and the side of the head, about halfway down the ear.

ARMS (MAKE 2):

Using White yarn:

Round 1: Sc 6 in a magic ring. [6 sts]

Round 2: Inc around. [12 sts]

Round 3: *Sc 3, inc; rep from * 2 more times. [15 sts]

Rounds 4–6: Sc around. [15 sts]

Round 7: Dec 6, sc 3. [9 sts]

Rounds 8–13: Sc around. [9 sts]

Finish off, leaving a long end. Stuff the hand and lower arm firmly, and stuff the upper arm more lightly. Press the open edges together to flatten the top of the arm, making sure that the hand curves inward. Sew straight across the opening to close it up, and then sew the arms to the sides of the body a couple of rounds below the neck.

LEGS (MAKE 2):

Using White yarn:

Round 1: Sc 6 in a magic ring. [6 sts]

Round 2: Inc around. [12 sts]

Round 3: *Sc, inc; rep from * 5 more times. [18 sts]

Rounds 4–6: Sc around. [18 sts]

Round 7: Dec 6, sc 6. [12 sts]

Rounds 8–11: Sc around. [12 sts]

Finish off, leaving a long end. Stuff the foot and lower leg firmly, and stuff the upper leg more lightly. Sew the legs to the front of the body, making sure that the feet curve upward.

TAIL:

Using White yarn:

Round 1: Sc 6 in a magic ring. [6 sts]

Round 2: Inc around. [12 sts]

Rounds 3–5: Sc around. [12 sts]

Round 6: Dec around. [6 sts]

Finish off, leaving a long end. Stuff the tail and sew it to the bottom back of the body.

CLEO THE CLEVER CAT

Cleo is living her best life in Cairo, enjoying the attentions of her adoring human and spending her days lounging in the hot Egyptian sun. When she isn't sleeping or curling up with her human on the couch, she puts her clever mind to work coming up with plans to thwart the overexcited poodle next door.

Size: 6 inches high

MATERIALS:

Bernat Super Value medium 4 (100% acrylic; 426 yards (389 m)/197 g): Natural, 90 yards

Walnut, 36 yards

US size G-6 (4.00 mm) crochet hook

2 (12-mm) black safety eyes

1 (15-mm) pink safety nose

Polyester fiberfill

Tapestry needle

Removable stitch marker

STITCHES USED:

Magic ring

Single crochet (sc)

Increase (inc)

Decrease (dec)

HEAD AND BODY:

The head and body are worked in one continuous piece, starting at the top of the head.

Using Natural yarn:

Round 1: Sc 6 in a magic ring. [6 sts]

Round 2: Inc around. [12 sts]

Round 3: *Sc, inc; rep from * 5 more times. [18 sts]

Round 4: *Sc 2, inc; rep from * 5 more times. [24 sts]

Round 5: *Sc 3, inc; rep from * 5 more times. [30 sts]

Round 6: *Sc 4, inc; rep from * 5 more times. [36 sts]

Round 7: *Sc 5, inc; rep from * 5 more times. [42 sts]

Rounds 8–16: Sc around. [42 sts]

Round 17: *Sc 5, dec; rep from * 5 more times. [36 sts]

Round 18: *Sc 4, dec; rep from * 5 more times. [30 sts]

Insert the safety eyes between Rounds 11 and 12, about six stitches apart. Insert the safety nose between Rounds 14 and 15 and centered between the eyes. Begin stuffing the head and continue to add stuffing as you crochet the remaining rounds.

Round 19: *Sc 3, dec; rep from * 5 more times. [24 sts]

Round 20: *Sc 2, dec; rep from * 5 more times. [18 sts]

Round 21: *Sc, dec; rep from * 5 more times. [12 sts]

Round 22: *Sc, inc; rep from * 5 more times. [18 sts]

Round 23: *Sc 2, inc; rep from * 5 more times. [24 sts]

Round 24: Sc around. [24 sts]

Round 25: *Sc 3, inc; rep from * 5 more times. [30 sts]

Round 26: Sc around. [30 sts]

Round 27: *Sc 4, inc; rep from * 5 more times. [36 sts]

Rounds 28–34: Sc around. [36 sts]

Round 35: *Sc 4, dec; rep from * 5 more times. [30 sts]

Round 36: *Sc 3, dec; rep from * 5 more times. [24 sts]

Round 37: *Sc 2, dec; rep from * 5 more times. [18 sts]

Round 38: *Sc, dec; rep from * 5 more times. [12 sts]

Round 39: Dec around. [6 sts]

Finish off and sew up the hole. Cut a length of walnut yarn and embroider whiskers on either side of the nose.

EARS (MAKE 2):

Using Walnut yarn:

Round 1: Sc 4 in a magic ring. [4 sts]

Round 2: *Sc, inc; rep from * 1 more time. [6 sts]

Round 3: *Sc 2, inc; rep from * 1 more time. [8 sts]

Round 4: *Sc 3, inc; rep from * 1 more time. [10 sts]

Round 5: *Sc 4, inc; rep from * 1 more time. [12 sts]

Round 6: *Sc 5, inc; rep from * 1 more time. [14 sts]

Round 7: *Sc 6, inc; rep from * 1 more time. [16 sts]

Finish off, leaving a long end. Do not stuff. Instead, press the open edges together to flatten the ear, and then sew straight across the opening to close it up. Sew the ears to the top front of the head, below Round 3.

ARMS (MAKE 2):

Using Walnut yarn:

Round 1: Sc 6 in a magic ring. [6 sts]

Round 2: Inc around. [12 sts]

Round 3: *Sc 3, inc; rep from * 2 more times. [15 sts]

Rounds 4–6: Sc around. [15 sts]

Round 7: Dec 6, sc 3. [9 sts]

Switch to Natural yarn:

Rounds 8–13: Sc around. [9 sts]

Finish off, leaving a long end. Stuff the hand and lower arm firmly, and stuff the upper arm more lightly. Press the open edges together to flatten the top of the arm, making sure that the hand curves inward. Sew straight across the opening to close it up, and then sew the arms to the sides of the body a couple of rounds below the neck.

LEGS (MAKE 2):

Using Walnut yarn:

Round 1: Sc 6 in a magic ring. [6 sts]

Round 2: Inc around. [12 sts]

Round 3: *Sc, inc; rep from * 5 more times. [18 sts]

Rounds 4–6: Sc around. [18 sts]

Round 7: Dec 6, sc 6. [12 sts]

Switch to Natural yarn:

Rounds 8–11: Sc around. [12 sts]

Finish off, leaving a long end. Stuff the foot and lower leg firmly, and stuff the upper leg more lightly. Sew the legs to the front of the body, making sure that the feet curve upward.

TAIL:

Stuff the tail lightly as you go.

Using Walnut yarn:

Round 1: Sc 6 in a magic ring. [6 sts]

Rounds 2–6: Sc around. [6 sts]

Switch to Natural yarn:

Rounds 7–21: Sc around. [6 sts]

Finish off, leaving a long end. Sew the tail to the back bottom of the body. Optionally, you can secure the tail to the body so that it stands up and doesn't stick out. Cut a length of natural yarn and make a few stitches between the inner edge of the tail and the back of the body, stitching up from the base of the tail for about 1 inch.

RENÉ THE RESTLESS RACCOON

René and his friends spend their nights roaming the neighborhoods of Montreal, stealing food and generally causing trouble. Knocking over trash cans was fun for a while, but the truth is René is getting restless. He isn't sure what he wants out of life yet, but he knows he needs a break from the same old nightly routine.

Size: 6½ inches high

MATERIALS:

Bernat Super Value medium 4 (100% acrylic; 426 yards (389 m)/197 g):
   True Gray, 100 yards

Black, 38 yards

White, 10 yards

US size G-6 (4.00 mm) crochet hook

2 (12-mm) black safety eyes

1 (15-mm) black safety nose

Polyester fiberfill

Tapestry needle

Removable stitch marker

STITCHES USED:

Magic ring

Chain (ch)

Slip stitch (sl st)

Single crochet (sc)

Half double crochet (hdc)

Double crochet (dc)

Increase (inc)

Decrease (dec)

In this pattern, you will learn how to make the oval shape of René's eyes by working around both sides of a foundation chain.

HEAD AND BODY:

The head and body are worked in one continuous piece, starting at the top of the head.

Using True Gray yarn:

Round 1: Sc 6 in a magic ring. [6 sts]

Round 2: Inc around. [12 sts]

Round 3: *Sc, inc; rep from * 5 more times. [18 sts]

Round 4: *Sc 2, inc; rep from * 5 more times. [24 sts]

Round 5: *Sc 3, inc; rep from * 5 more times. [30 sts]

Round 6: *Sc 4, inc; rep from * 5 more times. [36 sts]

Round 7: *Sc 5, inc; rep from * 5 more times. [42 sts]

Rounds 8–16: Sc around. [42 sts]

Round 17: *Sc 5, dec; rep from * 5 more times. [36 sts]

Round 18: *Sc 4, dec; rep from * 5 more times. [30 sts]

Begin stuffing the head and continue to add stuffing as you crochet the remaining rounds.

Round 19: *Sc 3, dec; rep from * 5 more times. [24 sts]

Round 20: *Sc 2, dec; rep from * 5 more times. [18 sts]

Round 21: *Sc, dec; rep from * 5 more times. [12 sts]

Round 22: *Sc, inc; rep from * 5 more times. [18 sts]

Round 23: *Sc 2, inc; rep from * 5 more times. [24 sts]

Round 24: Sc around. [24 sts]

Round 25: *Sc 3, inc; rep from * 5 more times. [30 sts]

Round 26: Sc around. [30 sts]

Round 27: *Sc 4, inc; rep from * 5 more times. [36 sts]

Rounds 28–34: Sc around. [36 sts]

Round 35: *Sc 4, dec; rep from * 5 more times. [30 sts]

Round 36: *Sc 3, dec; rep from * 5 more times. [24 sts]

Round 37: *Sc 2, dec; rep from * 5 more times. [18 sts]

Round 38: *Sc, dec; rep from * 5 more times. [12 sts]

Round 39: Dec around. [6 sts]

Finish off and sew up the hole.

RIGHT EYE:

Each eye patch starts with a foundation chain, and you will work into both sides of the chain to form an oval shape. The right and left eye patches are mirror images of each other, as seen from the raccoon's perspective. His right eye is on your left if you are looking at him, and vice versa. Work in a continuous spiral.

Insert a stitch marker into the first dc of Round 1.

Using Black yarn:

Ch 12

Round 1: Dc into fourth ch from hook, then in the remaining ch sts, dc 2, hdc 3, sc 3. [9 sts]

Round 2: Rotate your work so the other side of the foundation chain now faces up. Work into the loops on the other side of the chain,

including into the three ch sts that you skipped in Round 1: Sc 3, hdc 3, dc 6. [12 sts]

Switch to White yarn, leaving a long black end:

Round 3: Dc 3, hdc 3, sc 3. [9 sts]

Finish off, leaving a long white end. Insert the safety eye through one of the dc gaps at the wider end of the eye patch. Set aside and make the left eye.

LEFT EYE:

The left eye is a mirrored version of the right eye. You will start with a foundation chain of eleven stitches (instead of twelve stitches) and begin with the sc stitches. Using this method, the wide end will still be on the correct side and the white stripe will be on top.

Insert a stitch marker into the first sc of Round 1.

Using Black yarn:

Ch 11

Round 1: Sc 1 into second ch from hook, then in the remaining ch sts, sc 2, hdc 3, dc 4. [10 sts]

Round 2: Rotate your work so the other side of the foundation chain now faces up. Work into the loops on the other side of the chain, including into the one ch st that you skipped at the start of Round 1: Dc 5, hdc 3, sc 3. [11 sts]

Switch to White yarn, leaving a long black end:

Round 3: Sc 3, hdc 3, dc 3. [9 sts]

Sl st to finish off, leaving a long white end. Insert the safety eye through one of the dc gaps at the wider end of the eye patch.

Sew the eye patches to the face below Round 8. They should be positioned a few stitches apart, slanting downward, with the white stripe on top. Use the black ends to sew the black sections down and use the white ends to sew the white sections down. This ensures that the sewing stitches will not be visible.

SNOUT:

Using White yarn:

Round 1: Sc 6 in a magic ring. [6 sts]

Round 2: *Sc, inc; rep from * 2 more times. [9 sts]

Round 3: *Sc 2, inc; rep from * 2 more times. [12 sts]

Round 4: *Sc 3, inc; rep from * 2 more times. [15 sts]

Round 5: *Sc 4, inc; rep from * 2 more times. [18 sts]

Round 6: *Sc 5, inc; rep from * 2 more times. [21 sts]

Finish off, leaving a long end. Insert the safety nose between Rounds 1 and 2. The flat part of the nose should be facing up, and the bottom of the nose should be pointing down to the middle hole from Round 1. Stuff the snout, and then sew it to the front of the head just beneath the eyes. Make sure the snout is positioned so that the nose is facing up.

EARS (MAKE 2):

Using True Gray yarn:

Round 1: Sc 4 in a magic ring. [4 sts]

Round 2: *Sc, inc; rep from * 1 more time. [6 sts]

Round 3: *Sc 2, inc; rep from * 1 more time. [8 sts]

Round 4: *Sc 3, inc; rep from * 1 more time. [10 sts]

Round 5: *Sc 4, inc; rep from * 1 more time. [12 sts]

Round 6: *Sc 5, inc; rep from * 1 more time. [14 sts]

Round 7: *Sc 6, inc; rep from * 1 more time. [16 sts]

Finish off, leaving a long end. Do not stuff. Instead, press the open edges together to flatten the ear, and then sew straight across the opening to close it up. Sew the ears to the top front of the head, below Round 3.

ARMS (MAKE 2):

Using Black yarn:

Round 1: Sc 6 in a magic ring. [6 sts]

Round 2: Inc around. [12 sts]

Round 3: *Sc 3, inc; rep from * 2 more times. [15 sts]

Rounds 4–6: Sc around. [15 sts]

Round 7: Dec 6, sc 3. [9 sts]

Switch to True Gray yarn:

Rounds 8–13: Sc around. [9 sts]

Finish off, leaving a long end. Stuff the hand and lower arm firmly, and stuff the upper arm more lightly. Press the open edges together to flatten the top of the arm, making sure that the hand curves inward. Sew straight across the opening to close it up, and then sew the arms to the sides of the body a couple of rounds below the neck.

LEGS (MAKE 2):

Using Black yarn:

Round 1: Sc 6 in a magic ring. [6 sts]

Round 2: Inc around. [12 sts]

Round 3: *Sc, inc; rep from * 5 more times. [18 sts]

Rounds 4–6: Sc around. [18 sts]

Round 7: Dec 6, sc 6. [12 sts]

Switch to True Gray yarn:

Rounds 8–11: Sc around. [12 sts]

Finish off, leaving a long end. Stuff the foot and lower leg firmly, and stuff the upper leg more lightly. Sew the legs to the front of the body, making sure that the feet curve upward.

TAIL:

Using Black yarn:

Round 1: Sc 6 in a magic ring. [6 sts]

Round 2: *Sc, inc; rep from * 2 more times. [9 sts]

Round 3: *Sc 2, inc; rep from * 2 more times. [12 sts]

Switch to True Gray yarn:

Round 4: *Sc 3, inc; rep from * 2 more times. [15 sts]

Round 5: *Sc 4, inc; rep from * 2 more times. [18 sts]

Round 6: Sc around. [18 sts]

Switch to Black yarn:

Rounds 7–9: Sc around. [18 sts]

Switch to True Gray yarn:

Round 10: *Sc 4, dec; rep from * 2 more times. [15 sts]

Rounds 11–12: Sc around. [15 sts]

Begin stuffing the tail and continue to add stuffing as you crochet the remaining rounds.

Switch to Black yarn:

Round 13: *Sc 3, dec; rep from * 2 more times. [12 sts]

Rounds 14–15: Sc around. [12 sts]

Switch to True Gray yarn:

Round 16: *Sc 2, dec; rep from * 2 more times. [9 sts]

Rounds 17–18: Sc around. [9 sts]

Finish off, leaving a long end. Sew the tail to the bottom back of the body.

SOFIA THE SLEEPY SLOTH

Sofia enjoys lots of different hobbies in her Costa Rican jungle home. Sleeping is her favorite, but napping is a close second. Snoozing is fun, too, and of course who doesn't love the occasional siesta? Sometimes Sofia dreams about trying something new, perhaps pottery or yoga, but by the time she's woken up and eaten a few leaves, it's time for another nap!

Sofia and the next four patterns all use the same basic head, body, and limb shapes, with variations to their additional features such as faces, ears, and snouts. Sofia's eyes are made using the same technique as René the Restless Raccoon's eyes.

Size: 9 inches high

MATERIALS:

Bernat Super Value medium 4 (100% acrylic; 426 yards (389 m)/197 g):
  Taupe, 280 yards

Bernat Super Value yarn in Natural, 10 yards

Bernat Super Value yarn in Chocolate, 10 yards

US size G-6 (4.00 mm) crochet hook

2 (12-mm) black safety eyes

1 (18-mm) black safety nose

Polyester fiberfill

Tapestry needle

Removable stitch marker

STITCHES USED:

Magic ring

Chain (ch)

Slip stitch (sl st)

Single crochet (sc)

Half double crochet (hdc)

Double crochet (dc)

Increase (inc)

Decrease (dec)

HEAD AND BODY:

The head and body are worked in one continuous piece, starting at the top of the head.

Using Taupe yarn:

Round 1: Sc 6 in a magic ring. [6 sts]

Round 2: Inc around. [12 sts]

Round 3: *Sc, inc; rep from * 5 more times. [18 sts]

Round 4: *Sc 2, inc; rep from * 5 more times. [24 sts]

Round 5: *Sc 3, inc; rep from * 5 more times. [30 sts]

Round 6: *Sc 4, inc; rep from * 5 more times. [36 sts]

Round 7: *Sc 5, inc; rep from * 5 more times. [42 sts]

Round 8: *Sc 6, inc; rep from * 5 more times. [48 sts]

Round 9: *Sc 7, inc; rep from * 5 more times. [54 sts]

Rounds 10–19: Sc around. [54 sts]

Round 20: *Sc 7, dec; rep from * 5 more times. [48 sts]

Round 21: *Sc 6, dec; rep from * 5 more times. [42 sts]

Round 22: *Sc 5, dec; rep from * 5 more times. [36 sts]

Round 23: *Sc 4, dec; rep from * 5 more times. [30 sts]

Round 24: *Sc 3, dec; rep from * 5 more times. [24 sts]

Begin stuffing the head. After the next round, you will begin increasing to create the body. Once you've crocheted a few rounds of the body, finish stuffing the head and make sure that the neck area is stuffed firmly.

Round 25: *Sc 2, dec; rep from * 5 more times. [18 sts]

Round 26: *Sc 2, inc; rep from * 5 more times. [24 sts]

Round 27: *Sc 3, inc; rep from * 5 more times. [30 sts]

Round 28: *Sc 4, inc; rep from * 5 more times. [36 sts]

Round 29: Sc around. [36 sts]

Round 30: *Sc 5, inc; rep from * 5 more times. [42 sts]

Round 31: Sc around. [42 sts]

Round 32: *Sc 6, inc; rep from * 5 more times. [48 sts]

Round 33: Sc around. [48 sts]

Round 34: *Sc 7, inc; rep from * 5 more times. [54 sts]

Round 35: Sc around. [54 sts]

Round 36: *Sc 8, inc; rep from * 5 more times. [60 sts]

Rounds 37–49: Sc around. [60 sts]

Round 50: *Sc 8, dec; rep from * 5 more times. [54 sts]

Round 51: *Sc 7, dec; rep from * 5 more times. [48 sts]

Round 52: *Sc 6, dec; rep from * 5 more times. [42 sts]

Round 53: *Sc 5, dec; rep from * 5 more times. [36 sts]

Round 54: *Sc 4, dec; rep from * 5 more times. [30 sts]

Stuff the body. Continue to add stuffing as you crochet the remaining rounds.

Round 55: *Sc 3, dec; rep from * 5 more times. [24 sts]

Round 56: *Sc 2, dec; rep from * 5 more times. [18 sts]

Round 57: *Sc, dec; rep from * 5 more times. [12 sts]

Round 58: Dec around. [6 sts]

Finish off and sew up the hole.

FACE PATCH:

Using Natural yarn:

Round 1: Sc 6 in a magic ring. [6 sts]

Round 2: Inc around. [12 sts]

Round 3: *Sc, inc; rep from * 5 more times. [18 sts]

Round 4: *Sc 2, inc; rep from * 5 more times. [24 sts]

Round 5: *Sc 3, inc; rep from * 5 more times. [30 sts]

Round 6: *Sc 4, inc; rep from * 5 more times. [36 sts]

Round 7: *Sc 5, inc; rep from * 5 more times. [42 sts]

Round 8: *Sc 6, inc; rep from * 5 more times. [48 sts]

Finish off, leaving a long end. Insert the safety nose into the lower half of the face patch, between Rounds 3 and 4. The flat part of the nose should be facing up toward the middle of the face patch. Sew the face patch to the head.

EYES (MAKE 2):

Using Chocolate yarn:

Each eye patch starts with a foundation chain of 12 sts. You will work into both sides of the chain to form an oval shape. Work in a continuous spiral and insert a stitch marker into the first dc of Round 1. Reference photos for this technique are included in René the Restless Raccoon.

Ch 12

Round 1: Dc into the fourth ch from the hook, then in the remaining ch sts, dc 2, hdc 3, sc 3. [9 sts]

Round 2: Rotate your work so the other side of the foundation chain now faces up. Work into the loops on the other side of the chain, including into the three ch sts that you skipped at the start of Round 1: Sc 3, hdc 3, dc 6. [12 sts]

Round 3: Dc 3, hdc 3, sc 3. [9 sts]

Finish off, leaving a long end. Insert the safety eye through one of the dc gaps at the wider end of the eye patch. Sew the eye patches to the face. They should be positioned a few stitches apart, slanting downward over the edge of the face patch.

ARMS (MAKE 2):

Using Taupe yarn:

Round 1: Sc 6 in a magic ring. [6 sts]

Round 2: Inc around. [12 sts]

Round 3: *Sc, inc; rep from * 5 more times. [18 sts]

Round 4: *Sc 2, inc; rep from * 5 more times. [24 sts]

Rounds 5–9: Sc around. [24 sts]

Round 10: Dec 6, sc 12. [18 sts]

Rounds 11–28: Sc around. [18 sts]

Finish off, leaving a long tail. Stuff the hand and lower arm firmly, and stuff the upper arm more lightly. Press the open edges together to flatten the top of the arm, making sure that the hand curves inward. Sew straight across the opening to close it up, and then sew the arms to the sides of the body a couple of rounds below the neck.

LEGS (MAKE 2):

Using Taupe yarn:

Round 1: Sc 6 in a magic ring. [6 sts]

Round 2: Inc around. [12 sts]

Round 3: *Sc, inc; rep from * 5 more times. [18 sts]

Round 4: *Sc 2, inc; rep from * 5 more times. [24 sts]

Round 5: *Sc 7, inc; rep from * 2 more times. [27 sts]

Rounds 6–11: Sc around. [27 sts]

Round 12: Dec 6, sc 15. [21 sts]

Rounds 13–28: Sc around. [21 sts]

Finish off, leaving a long end. Stuff the foot and lower leg firmly, and stuff the upper leg more lightly. Sew the legs to the front of the body, making sure that the feet curve upward.

PING THE PEACEFUL PANDA

Ping's life in the forests of China is simple and quiet, which is exactly how he likes it. Other animals may find it boring and lonely, but Ping is a loner at heart and has always preferred solitude. After all, who needs a busy social life when there's bamboo to eat and naps to take? Ping is an easy and cuddly pattern, and he will make the perfect gift for anyone who loves pandas.

Size: 10½ inches high

MATERIALS:

Bernat Super Value medium 4 (100% acrylic; 426 yards (389 m)/197 g): White, 150 yards

Black, 190 yards

US size G-6 (4.00 mm) crochet hook

2 (12-mm) black safety eyes

1 (18-mm) black safety nose

Polyester fiberfill

Tapestry needle

Removable stitch marker

STITCHES USED:

Magic ring

Single crochet (sc)

Increase (inc)

Decrease (dec)

HEAD AND BODY:

The head and body are worked in one continuous piece, starting at the top of the head.

Using White yarn:

Round 1: Sc 6 in a magic ring. [6 sts]

Round 2: Inc around. [12 sts]

Round 3: *Sc, inc; rep from * 5 more times. [18 sts]

Round 4: *Sc 2, inc; rep from * 5 more times. [24 sts]

Round 5: *Sc 3, inc; rep from * 5 more times. [30 sts]

Round 6: *Sc 4, inc; rep from * 5 more times. [36 sts]

Round 7: *Sc 5, inc; rep from * 5 more times. [42 sts]

Round 8: *Sc 6, inc; rep from * 5 more times. [48 sts]

Round 9: *Sc 7, inc; rep from * 5 more times. [54 sts]

Rounds 10–19: Sc around. [54 sts]

Round 20: *Sc 7, dec; rep from * 5 more times. [48 sts]

Round 21: *Sc 6, dec; rep from * 5 more times. [42 sts]

Round 22: *Sc 5, dec; rep from * 5 more times. [36 sts]

Round 23: *Sc 4, dec; rep from * 5 more times. [30 sts]

Round 24: *Sc 3, dec; rep from * 5 more times. [24 sts]

Begin stuffing the head. After the next round, you will begin increasing to create the body. Once you've crocheted a few rounds of the body, finish stuffing the head and make sure that the neck area is stuffed firmly.

Round 25: *Sc 2, dec; rep from * 5 more times. [18 sts]

Change to Black yarn:

Round 26: *Sc 2, inc; rep from * 5 more times. [24 sts]

Round 27: *Sc 3, inc; rep from * 5 more times. [30 sts]

Round 28: *Sc 4, inc; rep from * 5 more times. [36 sts]

Round 29: Sc around. [36 sts]

Round 30: *Sc 5, inc; rep from * 5 more times. [42 sts]

Round 31: Sc around. [42 sts]

Round 32: *Sc 6, inc; rep from * 5 more times. [48 sts]

Round 33: Sc around. [48 sts]

Change to White yarn:

Round 34: *Sc 7, inc; rep from * 5 more times. [54 sts]

Round 35: Sc around. [54 sts]

Round 36: *Sc 8, inc; rep from * 5 more times. [60 sts]

Rounds 37–49: Sc around. [60 sts]

Round 50: *Sc 8, dec; rep from * 5 more times. [54 sts]

Round 51: *Sc 7, dec; rep from * 5 more times. [48 sts]

Round 52: *Sc 6, dec; rep from * 5 more times. [42 sts]

Round 53: *Sc 5, dec; rep from * 5 more times. [36 sts]

Round 54: *Sc 4, dec; rep from * 5 more times. [30 sts]

Stuff the body. Continue to add stuffing as you crochet the remaining rounds.

Round 55: *Sc 3, dec; rep from * 5 more times. [24 sts]

Round 56: *Sc 2, dec; rep from * 5 more times. [18 sts]

Round 57: *Sc, dec; rep from * 5 more times. [12 sts]

Round 58: Dec around. [6 sts]

Finish off and sew up the hole.

EYES (MAKE 2):

Using Black yarn:

Round 1: Sc 6 in a magic ring. [6 sts]

Round 2: Inc around. [12 sts]

Round 3: *Sc, inc; rep from * 5 more times. [18 sts]

Round 4: *Sc 2, inc; rep from * 5 more times. [24 sts]

Finish off, leaving a long end. Insert the safety eyes through the middle of each eye and secure with the safety eye washers. Sew the eyes to the head below Round 9. The eyes should be spaced about three or four stitches apart.

SNOUT:

Using White yarn:

Round 1: Sc 6 in a magic ring. [6 sts]

Round 2: Inc around. [12 sts]

Round 3: *Sc, inc; rep from * 5 more times. [18 sts]

Round 4: *Sc 2, inc; rep from * 5 more times. [24 sts]

Round 5: *Sc 3, inc; rep from * 5 more times. [30 sts]

Rounds 6–9: Sc around. [30 sts]

Finish off, leaving a long end. Insert the safety nose between Rounds 3 and 4. The flat part of the nose should be facing up, and the bottom of the nose should be pointing down to the middle hole from Round 1. Stuff the snout, then sew it to the face, slightly overlapping the bottoms of the eyes. Continue to add more stuffing to the snout as you sew it on.

EARS (MAKE 2):

Using Black yarn:

Round 1: Sc 6 in a magic ring. [6 sts]

Round 2: Inc around. [12 sts]

Round 3: *Sc, inc; rep from * 5 more times. [18 sts]

Round 4: *Sc 2, inc; rep from * 5 more times. [24 sts]

Rounds 5–10: Sc around. [24 sts]

Round 11: *Sc 2, dec; rep from * 5 more times. [18 sts]

Finish off, leaving a long end. Do not stuff. Instead, press the sides of the open edges together to flatten the ear, and then sew straight across the opening to close it up. Sew the ears to the head in a curved position, below Round 5.

ARMS (MAKE 2):

Using Black yarn:

Round 1: Sc 6 in a magic ring. [6 sts]

Round 2: Inc around. [12 sts]

Round 3: *Sc, inc; rep from * 5 more times. [18 sts]

Round 4: *Sc 2, inc; rep from * 5 more times. [24 sts]

Rounds 5–9: Sc around. [24 sts]

Round 10: Dec 6, sc 12. [18 sts]

Rounds 11–28: Sc around. [18 sts]

Finish off, leaving a long tail. Stuff the hand and lower arm firmly, and stuff the upper arm more lightly. Press the open edges together to flatten the top of the arm, making sure that the hand curves inward. Sew straight across the opening to close it up, and then sew the arms to the sides of the body a couple of rounds below the neck.

LEGS (MAKE 2):

Using Black yarn:

Round 1: Sc 6 in a magic ring. [6 sts]

Round 2: Inc around. [12 sts]

Round 3: *Sc, inc; rep from * 5 more times. [18 sts]

Round 4: *Sc 2, inc; rep from * 5 more times. [24 sts]

Round 5: *Sc 7, inc; rep from * 2 more times. [27 sts]

Rounds 6–11: Sc around. [27 sts]

Round 12: Dec 6, sc 15. [21 sts]

Rounds 13–28: Sc around. [21 sts]

Finish off, leaving a long end. Stuff the foot and lower leg firmly, and stuff the upper leg more lightly. Sew the legs to the front of the body, making sure that the feet curve upward.

KURTIS THE CAREFREE KOALA

Kurtis is happiest when he is chilling out, eating eucalyptus leaves, and napping in his favorite tree along Australia's Gold Coast. Every day, tourists pass underneath with their surfboards on the way to the beach. Sometimes he envisions himself joining them and riding the waves together, but that would involve leaving his comfy tree, which sounds like far too much effort. Kurtis uses the same base pattern as the sloth and panda, with the addition of multicolored ears.

Size: 10 inches high

MATERIALS:

Bernat Super Value medium 4 (100% acrylic; 426 yards (389 m)/197 g): True Gray, 320 yards

Black, 10 yards

White, 25 yards

US size G-6 (4.00 mm) crochet hook

2 (12-mm) black safety eyes

Polyester fiberfill

Tapestry needle

Removable stitch marker

STITCHES USED:

Magic ring

Single crochet (sc)

Increase (inc)

Decrease (dec)

HEAD AND BODY:

The head and body are worked in one continuous piece, starting at the top of the head.

Using True Gray yarn:

Round 1: Sc 6 in a magic ring. [6 sts]

Round 2: Inc around. [12 sts]

Round 3: *Sc, inc; rep from * 5 more times. [18 sts]

Round 4: *Sc 2, inc; rep from * 5 more times. [24 sts]

Round 5: *Sc 3, inc; rep from * 5 more times. [30 sts]

Round 6: *Sc 4, inc; rep from * 5 more times. [36 sts]

Round 7: *Sc 5, inc; rep from * 5 more times. [42 sts]

Round 8: *Sc 6, inc; rep from * 5 more times. [48 sts]

Round 9: *Sc 7, inc; rep from * 5 more times. [54 sts]

Rounds 10–19: Sc around. [54 sts]

Insert the safety eyes between Rounds 13 and 14, about seven stitches apart.

Round 20: *Sc 7, dec; rep from * 5 more times. [48 sts]

Round 21: *Sc 6, dec; rep from * 5 more times. [42 sts]

Round 22: *Sc 5, dec; rep from * 5 more times. [36 sts]

Round 23: *Sc 4, dec; rep from * 5 more times. [30 sts]

Round 24: *Sc 3, dec; rep from * 5 more times. [24 sts]

Begin stuffing the head. After the next round, you will begin increasing to create the body. Once you've crocheted a few rounds of the body, finish stuffing the head and make sure that the neck area is stuffed firmly.

Round 25: *Sc 2, dec; rep from * 5 more times. [18 sts]

Round 26: *Sc 2, inc; rep from * 5 more times. [24 sts]

Round 27: *Sc 3, inc; rep from * 5 more times. [30 sts]

Round 28: *Sc 4, inc; rep from * 5 more times. [36 sts]

Round 29: Sc around. [36 sts]

Round 30: *Sc 5, inc; rep from * 5 more times. [42 sts]

Round 31: Sc around. [42 sts]

Round 32: *Sc 6, inc; rep from * 5 more times. [48 sts]

Round 33: Sc around. [48 sts]

Round 34: *Sc 7, inc; rep from * 5 more times. [54 sts]

Round 35: Sc around. [54 sts]

Round 36: *Sc 8, inc; rep from * 5 more times. [60 sts]

Rounds 37–49: Sc around. [60 sts]

Round 50: *Sc 8, dec; rep from * 5 more times. [54 sts]

Round 51: *Sc 7, dec; rep from * 5 more times. [48 sts]

Round 52: *Sc 6, dec; rep from * 5 more times. [42 sts]

Round 53: *Sc 5, dec; rep from * 5 more times. [36 sts]

Round 54: *Sc 4, dec; rep from * 5 more times. [30 sts]

Stuff the body. Continue to add stuffing as you crochet the remaining rounds.

Round 55: *Sc 3, dec; rep from * 5 more times. [24 sts]

Round 56: *Sc 2, dec; rep from * 5 more times. [18 sts]

Round 57: *Sc, dec; rep from * 5 more times. [12 sts]

Round 58: Dec around. [6 sts]

Finish off and sew up the hole.

NOSE:

Using Black yarn:

Round 1: Sc 6 in a magic ring. [6 sts]

Round 2: Inc around. [12 sts]

Round 3: Inc 3, sc 3, inc 3, sc 3. [18 sts]

Round 4: Sc 2, inc 2, sc 7, inc 2, sc 5. [22 sts]

Rounds 5–6: Sc around. [22 sts]

Finish off, leaving a long end. The nose will naturally have a slight oval shape to it because of the shaping in Rounds 3 and 4. Add some stuffing, pinch the sides of the nose together to exaggerate the oval shape, and then sew it vertically to the face about one row below the eyes. Continue to add more stuffing to the nose as you sew it on.

OUTER EARS (MAKE 2):

Using True Gray yarn:

Round 1: Sc 6 in a magic ring. [6 sts]

Round 2: Inc around. [12 sts]

Round 3: *Sc, inc; rep from * 5 more times. [18 sts]

Round 4: *Sc 2, inc; rep from * 5 more times. [24 sts]

Round 5: *Sc 3, inc; rep from * 5 more times. [30 sts]

Rounds 6–12: Sc around. [30 sts]

Round 13: *Sc 3, dec; rep from * 5 more times. [24 sts]

Round 14: *Sc 2, dec; rep from * 5 more times. [18 sts]

Finish off, leaving a long end, and set aside without stuffing.

INNER EARS (MAKE 2):

Using White yarn:

Round 1: Sc 6 in a magic ring. [6 sts]

Round 2: Inc around. [12 sts]

Round 3: *Sc, inc; rep from * 5 more times. [18 sts]

Round 4: *Sc 2, inc; rep from * 5 more times. [24 sts]

Finish off, leaving a long end.

Next, you will sew the white inner earpiece to the gray outer ear. Press the sides of the outer ear's open edges together to flatten the ear. The ear will naturally take on a bowl shape, which is correct. Place the inner earpiece into the "bowl" of the ear and carefully sew the two pieces together. Make sure that you only sew through the inner layer of the outer ear, so the white stitches do not show up on the outside of the ear. Work slowly and check with each stitch that you have not sewn through the outer layer of the ear by mistake.

Once the earpieces are sewn together, use the long end from the outer ear piece and sew straight across the opening to close it up. Sew the ears to the head in a curved position, below Round 7.

ARMS (MAKE 2):

Using True Gray yarn:

Round 1: Sc 6 in a magic ring. [6 sts]

Round 2: Inc around. [12 sts]

Round 3: *Sc, inc; rep from * 5 more times. [18 sts]

Round 4: *Sc 2, inc; rep from * 5 more times. [24 sts]

Rounds 5–9: Sc around. [24 sts]

Round 10: Dec 6, sc 12. [18 sts]

Rounds 11–28: Sc around. [18 sts]

Finish off, leaving a long tail. Stuff the hand and lower arm firmly, and stuff the upper arm more lightly. Press the open edges together to flatten the top of the arm, making sure that the hand curves inward. Sew straight across the opening to close it up, and then sew the arms to the sides of the body a couple of rounds below the neck.

LEGS (MAKE 2):

Using True Gray yarn:

Round 1: Sc 6 in a magic ring. [6 sts]

Round 2: Inc around. [12 sts]

Round 3: *Sc, inc; rep from * 5 more times. [18 sts]

Round 4: *Sc 2, inc; rep from * 5 more times. [24 sts]

Round 5: *Sc 7, inc; rep from * 2 more times. [27 sts]

Rounds 6–11: Sc around. [27 sts]

Round 12: Dec 6, sc 15. [21 sts]

Rounds 13–28: Sc around. [21 sts]

Finish off, leaving a long end. Stuff the foot and lower leg firmly, and stuff the upper leg more lightly. Sew the legs to the front of the body, making sure that the feet curve upward.

BELLY:

Using White yarn:

Round 1: Sc 6 in a magic ring. [6 sts]

Round 2: Inc around. [12 sts]

Round 3: *Sc, inc; rep from * 5 more times. [18 sts]

Round 4: *Sc 2, inc; rep from * 5 more times. [24 sts]

Round 5: *Sc 3, inc; rep from * 5 more times. [30 sts]

Round 6: *Sc 4, inc; rep from * 5 more times. [36 sts]

Round 7: *Sc 5, inc; rep from * 5 more times. [42 sts]

Round 8: *Sc 6, inc; rep from * 5 more times. [48 sts]

Finish off, leaving a very long tail. Sew the belly onto the body.

MANJEET THE MISCHIEVOUS MONKEY

Manjeet is a bit of a troublemaker, but he has a good heart and never takes his pranks too far. Every few nights he sneaks off from his family to visit the small village near his forest home in northern India. After a few happy hours playing tricks on the locals, he tires himself out and his mother finds him asleep in the village square the next morning.

Size: 10 inches high

MATERIALS:

Bernat Super Value medium 4 (100% acrylic; 426 yards (389 m)/197 g): Chocolate, 270 yards

Topaz, 110 yards

US size G-6 (4.00 mm) crochet hook

2 (12-mm) black safety eyes

1 (18-mm) black safety nose

Polyester fiberfill

Tapestry needle

Removable stitch marker

STITCHES USED:

Magic ring

Single crochet (sc)

Increase (inc)

Decrease (dec)

HEAD AND BODY:

The head and body are worked in one continuous piece, starting at the top of the head.

Round 1: Sc 6 in a magic ring. [6 sts]

Round 2: Inc around. [12 sts]

Round 3: *Sc, inc; rep from * 5 more times. [18 sts]

Round 4: *Sc 2, inc; rep from * 5 more times. [24 sts]

Round 5: *Sc 3, inc; rep from * 5 more times. [30 sts]

Round 6: *Sc 4, inc; rep from * 5 more times. [36 sts]

Round 7: *Sc 5, inc; rep from * 5 more times. [42 sts]

Round 8: *Sc 6, inc; rep from * 5 more times. [48 sts]

Round 9: *Sc 7, inc; rep from * 5 more times. [54 sts]

Rounds 10–19: Sc around. [54 sts]

Round 20: *Sc 7, dec; rep from * 5 more times. [48 sts]

Round 21: *Sc 6, dec; rep from * 5 more times. [42 sts]

Round 22: *Sc 5, dec; rep from * 5 more times. [36 sts]

Round 23: *Sc 4, dec; rep from * 5 more times. [30 sts]

Round 24: *Sc 3, dec; rep from * 5 more times. [24 sts]

Begin stuffing the head. After the next round, you will begin increasing to create the body. Once you've crocheted a few rounds of the body, finish stuffing the head and make sure that the neck area is stuffed firmly.

Round 25: *Sc 2, dec; rep from * 5 more times. [18 sts]

Round 26: *Sc 2, inc; rep from * 5 more times. [24 sts]

Round 27: *Sc 3, inc; rep from * 5 more times. [30 sts]

Round 28: *Sc 4, inc; rep from * 5 more times. [36 sts]

Round 29: Sc around. [36 sts]

Round 30: *Sc 5, inc; rep from * 5 more times. [42 sts]

Round 31: Sc around. [42 sts]

Round 32: *Sc 6, inc; rep from * 5 more times. [48 sts]

Round 33: Sc around. [48 sts]

Round 34: *Sc 7, inc; rep from * 5 more times. [54 sts]

Round 35: Sc around. [54 sts]

Round 36: *Sc 8, inc; rep from * 5 more times. [60 sts]

Rounds 37–49: Sc around. [60 sts]

Round 50: *Sc 8, dec; rep from * 5 more times. [54 sts]

Round 51: *Sc 7, dec; rep from * 5 more times. [48 sts]

Round 52: *Sc 6, dec; rep from * 5 more times. [42 sts]

Round 53: *Sc 5, dec; rep from * 5 more times. [36 sts]

Round 54: *Sc 4, dec; rep from * 5 more times. [30 sts]

Stuff the body. Continue to add stuffing as you crochet the remaining rounds.

Round 55: *Sc 3, dec; rep from * 5 more times. [24 sts]

Round 56: *Sc 2, dec; rep from * 5 more times. [18 sts]

Round 57: *Sc, dec; rep from * 5 more times. [12 sts]

Round 58: Dec around. [6 sts]

Finish off and close up the hole.

EYES (MAKE 2):

Using Topaz yarn:

Round 1: Sc 6 in a magic ring. [6 sts]

Round 2: Inc around. [12 sts]

Round 3: *Sc, inc; rep from * 5 more times. [18 sts]

Round 4: *Sc 2, inc; rep from * 5 more times. [24 sts]

Finish off, leaving a long end. Insert the safety eyes through the middle of each eye and secure with the safety eye washers. Sew the eyes to the head beneath Round 9. The eyes should be close together (just touching in the middle) and centered over the belly.

SNOUT:

Using Topaz yarn:

Round 1: Sc 6 in a magic ring. [6 sts]

Round 2: Inc around. [12 sts]

Round 3: *Sc, inc; rep from * 5 more times. [18 sts]

Round 4: *Sc 2, inc; rep from * 5 more times. [24 sts]

Round 5: *Sc 3, inc; rep from * 5 more times. [30 sts]

Rounds 6–9: Sc around. [30 sts]

Finish off, leaving a long end. Insert the safety nose between Rounds 3 and 4. The flat part of the nose should be facing up, and the bottom of the nose should be pointing down to the middle hole from Round 1. Stuff the snout, then sew it to the face, slightly overlapping the bottoms of the eyes. Continue to add more stuffing to the snout as you sew it on.

EARS (MAKE 2):

Using Topaz yarn:

Round 1: Sc 6 in a magic ring. [6 sts]

Round 2: Inc around. [12 sts]

Round 3: *Sc, inc; rep from * 5 more times. [18 sts]

Round 4: *Sc 2, inc; rep from * 5 more times. [24 sts]

Rounds 5–10: Sc around. [24 sts]

Round 11: *Sc 2, dec; rep from * 5 more times. [18 sts]

Round 12: *Sc, dec; rep from * 5 more times. [12 sts]

Finish off, leaving a long end. Do not stuff. Instead, press the sides of the open edges together to flatten the ear, and then sew straight across the opening to close it up. Sew the ears to the side of the head. The tops of the ears should be level with the tops of the eyes.

ARMS (MAKE 2):

Using Topaz yarn:

Round 1: Sc 6 in a magic ring. [6 sts]

Round 2: Inc around. [12 sts]

Round 3: *Sc, inc; rep from * 5 more times. [18 sts]

Round 4: *Sc 2, inc; rep from * 5 more times. [24 sts]

Rounds 5–8: Sc around. [24 sts]

Change to Chocolate yarn:

Round 9: Sc around. [24 sts]

Round 10: Dec 6, sc 12. [18 sts]

Rounds 11–28: Sc around. [18 sts]

Finish off, leaving a long tail. Stuff the hand and lower arm firmly, and stuff the upper arm more lightly. Press the open edges together to flatten the top of the arm, making sure that the hand curves inward. Sew straight across the opening to close it up, and then sew the arms to the sides of the body a couple of rounds below the neck.

LEGS (MAKE 2):

Using Topaz yarn:

Round 1: Sc 6 in a magic ring. [6 sts]

Round 2: Inc around. [12 sts]

Round 3: *Sc, inc; rep from * 5 more times. [18 sts]

Round 4: *Sc 2, inc; rep from * 5 more times. [24 sts]

Round 5: *Sc 7, inc; rep from * 2 more times. [27 sts]

Rounds 6–10: Sc around. [27 sts]

Change to Chocolate yarn:

Round 11: Sc around. [27 sts]

Round 12: Dec 6, sc 15. [21 sts]

Rounds 13–28: Sc around. [21 sts]

Finish off, leaving a long end. Stuff the foot and lower leg firmly, and stuff the upper leg more lightly. Sew the legs to the front of the body, making sure that the feet curve upward.

BELLY:

Using Topaz yarn:

Round 1: Sc 6 in a magic ring. [6 sts]

Round 2: Inc around. [12 sts]

Round 3: *Sc, inc; rep from * 5 more times. [18 sts]

Round 4: *Sc 2, inc; rep from * 5 more times. [24 sts]

Round 5: *Sc 3, inc; rep from * 5 more times. [30 sts]

Round 6: *Sc 4, inc; rep from * 5 more times. [36 sts]

Round 7: *Sc 5, inc; rep from * 5 more times. [42 sts]

Round 8: *Sc 6, inc; rep from * 5 more times. [48 sts]

Finish off, leaving a very long tail. Sew the belly onto the body.

TAIL:

Using Chocolate yarn:

Stuff the tail lightly as you crochet it. Don't leave the stuffing to the end, as it will be too difficult to stuff the long tail.

Round 1: Sc 6 in a magic ring. [6 sts]

Round 2: Inc around. [12 sts]

Rounds 3–50: Sc around. [12 sts]

Finish off, leaving a long end. Sew the tail to the back bottom of the body.

FERGUS THE FUN-LOVING FOX

Fergus is always up for playing a fun game, and most nights he can be found running around the Scottish Highlands searching for friends to join him. One night, he tried to convince the chickens at a nearby farm to play hide-and-seek, but they were afraid of Fergus and only wanted to hide. Fergus uses many of the same pattern elements as the last few projects, so if you've made the sloth, koala, panda, or monkey, then you shouldn't have any trouble making this adorable and cuddly fox.

Size: 9½ inches high

MATERIALS:
Bernat Super Value medium 4 (100% acrylic; 426 yards (389 m)/197 g): Carrot, 250 yards
White, 70 yards
Black, 70 yards
US size G-6 (4.00 mm) crochet hook
2 (12-mm) black safety eyes
1 (18-mm) black safety nose
Polyester fiberfill
Tapestry needle
Removable stitch marker

STITCHES USED:
Magic ring
Single crochet (sc)
Increase (inc)
Decrease (dec)

HEAD AND BODY:

The head and body are worked in one continuous piece, starting at the top of the head.

Using Carrot yarn:

Round 1: Sc 6 in a magic ring. [6 sts]

Round 2: Inc around. [12 sts]

Round 3: *Sc, inc; rep from * 5 more times. [18 sts]

Round 4: *Sc 2, inc; rep from * 5 more times. [24 sts]

Round 5: *Sc 3, inc; rep from * 5 more times. [30 sts]

Round 6: *Sc 4, inc; rep from * 5 more times. [36 sts]

Round 7: *Sc 5, inc; rep from * 5 more times. [42 sts]

Round 8: *Sc 6, inc; rep from * 5 more times. [48 sts]

Round 9: *Sc 7, inc; rep from * 5 more times. [54 sts]

Rounds 10–17: Sc around. [54 sts]

Switch to White yarn:

Rounds 18–19: Sc around. [54 sts]

Round 20: *Sc 7, dec; rep from * 5 more times. [48 sts]

Round 21: *Sc 6, dec; rep from * 5 more times. [42 sts]

Round 22: *Sc 5, dec; rep from * 5 more times. [36 sts]

Round 23: *Sc 4, dec; rep from * 5 more times. [30 sts]

Round 24: *Sc 3, dec; rep from * 5 more times. [24 sts]

Insert the safety eyes between Rounds 13 and 14, about seven stitches apart. Begin stuffing the head. After the next round, you will begin increasing to create the body. Once you've crocheted a few rounds of the body, finish stuffing the head and make sure that the neck area is stuffed firmly.

Round 25: *Sc 2, dec; rep from * 5 more times. [18 sts]

Switch to Carrot yarn:

Round 26: *Sc 2, inc; rep from * 5 more times. [24 sts]

Round 27: *Sc 3, inc; rep from * 5 more times. [30 sts]

Round 28: *Sc 4, inc; rep from * 5 more times. [36 sts]

Round 29: Sc around. [36 sts]

Round 30: *Sc 5, inc; rep from * 5 more times. [42 sts]

Round 31: Sc around. [42 sts]

Round 32: *Sc 6, inc; rep from * 5 more times. [48 sts]

Round 33: Sc around. [48 sts]

Round 34: *Sc 7, inc; rep from * 5 more times. [54 sts]

Round 35: Sc around. [54 sts]

Round 36: *Sc 8, inc; rep from * 5 more times. [60 sts]

Rounds 37–49: Sc around. [60 sts]

Round 50: *Sc 8, dec; rep from * 5 more times. [54 sts]

Round 51: *Sc 7, dec; rep from * 5 more times. [48 sts]

Round 52: *Sc 6, dec; rep from * 5 more times. [42 sts]

Round 53: *Sc 5, dec; rep from * 5 more times. [36 sts]

Round 54: *Sc 4, dec; rep from * 5 more times. [30 sts]

Stuff the body. Continue to add stuffing as you crochet the remaining rounds.

Round 55: *Sc 3, dec; rep from * 5 more times. [24 sts]

Round 56: *Sc 2, dec; rep from * 5 more times. [18 sts]

Round 57: *Sc, dec; rep from * 5 more times. [12 sts]

Round 58: Dec around. [6 sts]

Finish off and close up the hole.

SNOUT:

Using White yarn:

Round 1: Sc 6 in a magic ring. [6 sts]

Round 2: Inc around. [12 sts]

Round 3: Sc around. [12 sts]

Round 4: *Sc 3, inc; rep from * 2 more times. [15 sts]

Round 5: Sc around. [15 sts]

Insert the safety nose between Rounds 1 and 2. The flat part of the nose should be facing up, and the bottom of the nose should be pointing down to the middle hole from Round 1.

Round 6: *Sc 4, inc; rep from * 2 more times. [18 sts]

Round 7: Sc around. [18 sts]

Round 8: *Sc 5, inc; rep from * 2 more times. [21 sts]

Round 9: Sc around. [21 sts]

Round 10: *Sc 6, inc; rep from * 2 more times. [24 sts]

Round 11: Sc around. [24 sts]

Finish off, leaving a long end. Stuff the snout, and then sew it to the front of the head just beneath the eyes. Make sure the snout is positioned so that the nose is facing up.

EARS (MAKE 2):

Using Carrot yarn:

Round 1: Sc 4 in a magic ring. [4 sts]

Round 2: *Sc, inc; rep from * 1 more time. [6 sts]

Round 3: *Sc 2, inc; rep from * 1 more time. [8 sts]

Round 4: *Sc 3, inc; rep from * 1 more time. [10 sts]

Round 5: *Sc 4, inc; rep from * 1 more time. [12 sts]

Round 6: *Sc 5, inc; rep from * 1 more time. [14 sts]

Round 7: *Sc 6, inc; rep from * 1 more time. [16 sts]

Round 8: *Sc 7, inc; rep from * 1 more time. [18 sts]

Round 9: *Sc 8, inc; rep from * 1 more time. [20 sts]

Round 10: *Sc 9, inc; rep from * 1 more time. [22 sts]

Round 11: *Sc 10, inc; rep from * 1 more time. [24 sts]

Finish off, leaving a long end. Do not stuff. Instead, press the open edges together to flatten the ear, and then sew straight across the opening to close it up. Sew the ears to the top front of the head, below Round 3.

ARMS (MAKE 2):

Using Black yarn:

Round 1: Sc 6 in a magic ring. [6 sts]

Round 2: Inc around. [12 sts]

Round 3: *Sc, inc; rep from * 5 more times. [18 sts]

Round 4: *Sc 2, inc; rep from * 5 more times. [24 sts]

Rounds 5–8: Sc around. [24 sts]

Change to Carrot yarn:

Round 9: Sc around. [24 sts]

Round 10: Dec 6, sc 12. [18 sts]

Rounds 11–28: Sc around. [18 sts]

Finish off, leaving a long tail. Stuff the hand and lower arm firmly, and stuff the upper arm more lightly. Press the open edges together to flatten the top of the arm, making sure that the hand curves inward. Sew straight across the opening to close it up, and then sew the arms to the sides of the body a couple of rounds below the neck.

LEGS (MAKE 2):

Using Black yarn:

Round 1: Sc 6 in a magic ring. [6 sts]

Round 2: Inc around. [12 sts]

Round 3: *Sc, inc; rep from * 5 more times. [18 sts]

Round 4: *Sc 2, inc; rep from * 5 more times. [24 sts]

Round 5: *Sc 7, inc; rep from * 2 more times. [27 sts]

Rounds 6–10: Sc around. [27 sts]

Change to Carrot yarn:

Round 11: Sc around. [27 sts]

Round 12: Dec 6, sc 15. [21 sts]

Rounds 13–28: Sc around. [21 sts]

Finish off, leaving a long end. Stuff the foot and lower leg firmly, and stuff the upper leg more lightly. Sew the legs to the front of the body, making sure that the feet curve upward.

BELLY:

Using White yarn:

Round 1: Sc 6 in a magic ring. [6 sts]

Round 2: Inc around. [12 sts]

Round 3: *Sc, inc; rep from * 5 more times. [18 sts]

Round 4: *Sc 2, inc; rep from * 5 more times. [24 sts]

Round 5: *Sc 3, inc; rep from * 5 more times. [30 sts]

Round 6: *Sc 4, inc; rep from * 5 more times. [36 sts]

Round 7: *Sc 5, inc; rep from * 5 more times. [42 sts]

Round 8: *Sc 6, inc; rep from * 5 more times. [48 sts]

Finish off, leaving a very long tail. Sew the belly onto the body.

TAIL:

Using White yarn:

Round 1: Sc 6 in a magic ring. [6 sts]

Round 2: *Sc, inc; rep from * 2 more times. [9 sts]

Round 3: *Sc 2, inc; rep from * 2 more times. [12 sts]

Round 4: *Sc 3, inc; rep from * 2 more times. [15 sts]

Round 5: *Sc 4, inc; rep from * 2 more times. [18 sts]

Round 6: *Sc 5, inc; rep from * 2 more times. [21 sts]

Round 7: *Sc 6, inc; rep from * 2 more times. [24 sts]

Round 8: *Sc 7, inc; rep from * 2 more times. [27 sts]

Round 9: *Sc 8, inc; rep from * 2 more times. [30 sts]

Round 10: *Sc 9, inc; rep from * 2 more times. [33 sts]

Round 11: *Sc 10, inc; rep from * 2 more times. [36 sts]

Rounds 12–13: Sc around. [36 sts]

Switch to Carrot yarn:

Rounds 14–18: Sc around. [36 sts]

Round 19: *Sc 10, dec; rep from * 2 more times. [33 sts]

Round 20: Sc around. [33 sts]

Round 21: *Sc 9, dec; rep from * 2 more times. [30 sts]

Round 22: Sc around. [30 sts]

Begin stuffing the tail. Continue to add stuffing as you complete the remaining rounds.

Round 23: *Sc 8, dec; rep from * 2 more times. [27 sts]

Round 24: Sc around. [27 sts]

Round 25: *Sc 7, dec; rep from * 2 more times. [24 sts]

Round 26: Sc around. [24 sts]

Round 27: *Sc 6, dec; rep from * 2 more times. [21 sts]

Round 28: Sc around. [21 sts]

Round 29: *Sc 5, dec; rep from * 2 more times. [18 sts]

Round 30: Sc around. [18 sts]

Round 31: *Sc 4, dec; rep from * 2 more times. [15 sts]

Round 32: Sc around. [15 sts]

Finish off, leaving a long end. Sew the tail to the bottom back of the body.

Printed in Great Britain
by Amazon